Well-Versed
A **Powerful** Guide to **Business Success**

Well-Versed

A **Powerful** Guide to Business Success

David Adams

Well-Versed

A **Powerful** Guide to **Business Success**

First published in 2015 by
Panoma Press Ltd
48 St Vincent Drive, St Albans, Herts, AL1 5SJ UK

info@panomapress.com
www.panomapress.com

Cover design by Michael Inns
Artwork by Karen Gladwell

ISBN 978-1-909623-86-6

Contents

*"I am never weary of being useful... In serving others I cannot do enough.
No labour is sufficient to tire me."*
Leonardo da Vinci

Dedicated to everyone – clients and colleagues – that I have had the privilege to work with over the years and with whom I've been able to share what I've learned.

Acknowledgements

MANY PEOPLE have helped in the production of this book, both knowingly and unknowingly. I would like to thank the people who have helped me to understand what it means to be a business coach and those who by putting themselves in the business groups I have the privilege to chair, have themselves taught me the needs of business people. This is a quite different perspective from that of being a former CEO.

I am very grateful to those who commented on earlier drafts, some of them clients, some of them colleagues and some family and friends. In addition those who helped me to form my opinions, Steve Elson, Jo Haigh, Jeannette Hobson, Kasper Larsen, John Lee, Brian Marcel, Zanine Margetson, Andy Mintern, Dene Schofield, Nick Shanagher and Gisèle Waterman.

Special thanks to Mindy Gibbins-Klein, aka The Book Midwife, who guided me through the process and without whose strict mentoring, the whole thing would never have been achieved.

What readers have said:

"Tap into 40 years of unique business and life experience in the space of an afternoon."
Kasper Larsen,
CEO of world-leading statistics software company.

"I have been privileged to know David for many years as a colleague, a friend and a teacher. David will tell you just how it is and in such a way that although he is clearly not taking any prisoners you can't help but really like him for it. A great book with some insightful thoughts which leave you thinking: 'Well, maybe I'll try it this way and see what happens."
Jo Haigh,
corporate financier and author of numerous business books.

"David Adams captures the elements of business in a unique way so that the reader can see the rhythm, the creativity and the non-linear connections. A total surprise and an eye-opener."
Jeannette Hobson, business coach, New York City

Introduction

This
Is the overall
Concept
This
Is the essence
Of my thoughts
Of my breathing
Of my writings
I will try
To eloquently
Encapsulate
Some learnings
Some teachings
Some perfect
Processes
To enable
My readers
Achieve

Their constant
Dreams
Their constant
Vision, their constant
Goals and targets
For their success
Learnings from
My mentors
From my peers
From my judges
And also from those
With whom
I disagree
So that
In the end
I have developed
A best case
For your success in business

Introduction

A ramble through the woods of the mind; my background and influences. Before you read this book you need to understand how I came to be who I am and know what I know

I LOVE what I do and it's best to make sure that what you do is not only enjoyable but also successful. What will you find in this book? My aim is for it to be a business book with a difference; a business book you can dip into or read in its entirety. A business book with anecdotes, brief case stories and snippets to help aspiring business people grow their businesses as well as grow with their businesses.

I left school at 17 and trained to become a chartered accountant. At the same time, I dabbled with poetry. It was a great way to encourage girls which is more than could be said for accountancy. On the other hand, that professional qualification led to what I consider to be a successful career in stockbroking and later to my current activity, business and leadership coaching.

As a chief executive, I learnt the difference between being in business and running a business. I enjoyed the former rather than the latter although the company did prosper despite that lesser feeling. Many people these days start businesses because they love the idea of delivering a product or a service but as explained in The E-Myth, (Michael E Gerber) people don't realise the number of roles an entrepreneur must play to successfully build a business. More of that later.

Once I had spent eight years as CEO with my team taking the business to record profits, I had had enough (I had been there for 27 years!) and I felt that the company had had enough of me. I went to Loch Lomond in Scotland from my home in the south of Manchester and just wandered about. This was at the suggestion of a great Vistage speaker (see Chapter 11), Walt Sutton, a 'personal retreat' – three days of solitude and beauty in the wilds. Day one, wander about, not thinking, but giving the brain a break and later, after cleaning up and dinner with a good bottle of wine, take out the notebook and write down what one wants to achieve in life. Day two, same process but the notebook later that day was to contain what one wanted to achieve in the next five years. (Choose a timescale to suit you – I was coming up to age 50 at the time.) Day three, in the evening, notebook; imagine one had six months to live, what would be important? A wonderful exercise and one I have repeated over the years though at rather less cathartic times. As I drove home on the fourth day, it came into my head to leave, without actually doing anything about it. Within two weeks I was head-hunted and enticed to a similar role in London. Bottom line, I loved London and hated the job. Looking back, I think the board realised that the fit was less than perfect and very excitingly, I was fired! Possibly the best thing that ever happened to me in business.

As chief executive of the Manchester headquartered company, Henry Cooke Lumsden, I had become a member of a so-called 'peer' or mastermind group, at that time called TEC, now called Vistage. As a member of the group, I had a superb coach/mentor, Ivan Goldberg, and this helped me to teach myself much more about running a business and also about running myself. It was through Ivan that I met Walt. Ivan is still going strong as a coach facilitator with a great following.

Much later, about five years in fact, I met a poet, David Whyte, an Irish Yorkshireman, who had taken poetry to corporate America. He set me thinking. Further along the trail, I met two guys from San Francisco, Rick Martin and Ole Carlson, who showed me some exercises using poetry. The following year, my younger daughter Zanine, who was teaching food and beverage in Boston, MA, had taken a creative writing course. She wrote a poem for my birthday, which truly knocked me out and I realised just how powerful poetry could be. As Robert Frost (USA, 1874–1963) said "poetry grabs life by the throat". I rediscovered that I was able to write and started to put together the theme of helping business people by using poetry as a catalyst. Unfortunately I entitled my talks 'Poetry in Business' which was like putting up garlic to a vampire or Kryptonite to Superman, so I changed it to Unlocking Creativity™.

After leaving stockbroking, I set myself up as a consultant to professional practice, which is in effect what I had been part of and running for many years. I focused on the legal profession; why, I'm not sure and truly it was a disaster! Every firm I spoke to was either big enough to have realised that they did indeed need a chief executive, or smaller and fixated on the need to drive client fees. From what I can see, things haven't changed. I was fortunate that a former colleague was sitting on an advisory committee at The London Stock Exchange and they were deeply worried about AIM (the Alternative Investment Market). This is the junior stock market, which was then in its infancy and having a lot of teething troubles. They asked me to act as consultant, which I did for six months, interviewing all the NOMADs (nominated advisers). Subsequently the rules were changed and AIM took off in splendid fashion. The process also put me into contact with a great number of really useful and ultimately helpful individuals.

After this I was approached by a very old friend from Manchester, Harold Morley, who at the time was chairman of a medical technology company run by an Israeli immigrant, Tuvi Orbach. Tuvi had been head of systems in the IDF (Israeli Defence Forces). He had teamed up with a professor of medical electronics, Bernard Watson from Bart's Hospital in London and together they formed Ultramind, which was researching and developing the concept of driving computer animation using thought waves, a revolution at that time (1996). I spent two years helping the team grow the business, initially with the idea of floating. Later, we realised it was too cash-hungry and succeeded in selling to a listed company, where for a time the shares exploded on the back of the internet boom.

The Israeli half of the board – being rather more direct than the Brits – were quite amused when I first met them and was equivocal rather than giving a straight view about the company's prospects. They thought that stance was, in their words, "typically British" but there again as Alain de Botton has declared, "if Facebook had been developed in Britain, it would have had a 'quite like' button". Anyway, the successor to Ultramind eventually managed to bring a programme entitled "Beating the Blues" into the National Health Service, but it took six years to do so.

After that my friend and mentor, Ivan, called me up and asked me what I was going to do next and would I like to consider becoming a peer group chair? I said that sounded interesting and applied. After some time, I was recruited on a freelance basis to build a group and run it as facilitator coach. My success as a group builder was limited and eventually I was invited to take over a group where the existing chair wanted to reduce his activity. The group had twelve members at the time but I later discovered that five were in the process of selling up so I had to start recruiting like mad. I was lucky and built the group to 16, thinking that was it. I was wrong. That was fifteen years ago and at the time of writing I'm still building the group!

My childhood was relatively uneventful. For the first three years of my life, I was brought up by my virtually single parent mother while dad was an officer in the Royal Artillery in the latter part of WWII. As I had no siblings, I was adored and doted upon and of course as thoroughly spoilt as a wartime child could be. When dad came home, he started in business as textile merchant encouraged by a chartered accountant friend. He was a great salesman having won plaudits pre-war as top salesman at Averys, the weighing machine manufacturer (they're still around today, although, having been in and out of GEC, in a rather different incarnation, as Avery Weigh Tronix).

This family environment in business was, I feel, a great influence on me. It helped me realise the value and purpose of running one's own business and has helped me enormously in understanding SMEs (small and medium-sized enterprises). It was great fun for me growing up to watch and listen to my father doing deals in cloth with potential buyers sitting drinking coffee in the Kardomah. (They weren't called coffee shops in those days, but that's what they were.) It was hard for me to understand why a farthing (1/4 of an old penny, 960 to the pound) was so important. Incidentally, interesting how the businesses of insurance and stock broking, among others, started at the end of the 17th century; stock broking with Jonathan's Coffee House, when traders were expelled from the Royal Exchange for rowdiness (*plus ça change!* – another play on words as Jonathan's was situated in Change Alley) and now so much business is undertaken once again in Starbucks and Cafe Nero among others; as they say, "cheap office space, expensive coffee".

Watching my father deal in this way and later as I grew up learning the importance of actual cash in business was significant. As someone said it's easy to have cashless profit but difficult to have profitless cash. Dad turned his business from what was in effect credit drapery to a totally cash-focused business where he bought on credit and sold for cash. He managed that by building wonderful relationships over the years and commanded great respect in the business community. On many occasions, people would say to me, "oh, you're Bert's son, what a lovely man!"

Dad also taught me the lesson of succession planning. I think he would have liked me to have followed him into the business and as I grew up, I did spend quite a lot of time helping out, particularly in the warehouse at the weekends and in school holidays but he was also very keen on my obtaining a professional qualification after I left school. So, he found a chap, Barry Starr, whom he thought of as a second son and groomed him to take over the business when dad was not fit enough to continue, although he never actually retired.

That's something else I learned from him. Although I have a number of friends who claim to be very happy in retirement, I have the experience of seeing at least six close colleagues retire from Henry Cooke while I was CEO, who died within two years of so doing. On the other hand, a wonderful guy, Pat Hyndman, continued as a Vistage chair in San Diego till he was 96 and only died at the age of 98. He always said he wanted to be carried out on his flip chart. Not a bad act to follow!

One of the most influential people in my early life was my English schoolmaster, Brian Phythian. Not only did he help me get through English A level (no mean feat) but he was a terrific mentor, a brilliant actor. We all went to see him perform as Ham in Beckett's *Endgame* at Manchester Cathedral – and unusually for those days, even at Manchester Grammar School, he had a nurturing quality that made you want to learn. More importantly, he helped continue the success of the dramatic society, which not only produced Ben Kingsley but also Robert Powell, who while he tends now to concentrate on soap was a brilliant Christ (in the film *Jesus of Nazareth*, 1977). My claim to fame is having been on the same stage at the same time as both Jesus Christ and Mahatma Gandhi (played magnificently by the aforesaid Ben Kingsley). I was playing the nurse, Nérine, in Molière's Les Fourberies de Scapin at the time!

As a trainee accountant, I was fortunate enough to be allowed to take a few months off during my Articles (indentured training period) to work in the cost accounting department of the Dunlop Rubber Company in Manchester. This was an experience of its own. The company, the general rubber goods division, was housed in a 150-year-old factory in Cambridge Street. It had been the refuge of soldiers during the notorious Peterloo Massacre of pro-democracy and anti-poverty demonstrators on 16 August 1819 being very close to St Peter's Fields. The last time I was in Manchester this was a tram stop! Apart from being an awful place to work, it was an eye-opener for me. Raw rubber from the plantations came into the ground floor; it was then lowered two floors underground where the men were paid what was known as 'dirt money' – about an extra (old) penny an hour to handle this smelly and filthy raw material and cut it up into manageable chunks. It was then raised a few floors where it was made into goods ranging from tractor tyres to household rubber gloves; this latter was to my mind a thankless and boring task undertaken by ladies. I was told they enjoyed the routine! I hope things have changed but this was 1965. Anyway, the experience of working there, while it taught me a lot, put me off industry for life.

While I was preparing to take my finals I took extended study leave, as my five years was up. It wasn't all bad and I learned a lot going from business to business. A particular memory is that of a petrol filling station and car showroom on the outskirts of Bury. Apart from my father's business, it was the first family business I had come across. Mr X (I will call him that for reasons that will become clear), looked after the petrol and the cars while Mrs X worked at the top of a very narrow and steep staircase where she kept the books. The third character was a jet black mynah bird that screeched most of the time imitating the yelling that went on between Mr and Mrs. It was ostensibly there for security reasons but its swear word vocabulary was more extensive than mine. One morning my senior clerk Terry and I arrived to find Mrs being bodily thrown down the stairs by Mr, the result of the most violent and voluble altercation yet. By 'tea time' later that morning, they were all smiles again!

My training period also taught me three-card brag, a sort of mini poker. Fortunately I was good at this and it enabled me to take a girl out on Saturday evening, something that was quite difficult on £4 per week. (When I joined I was told that I was lucky; until a couple of years before, clerks paid a premium for their contract.) The other thing I was taught within a few days by one of the posher seniors from an upmarket part of Cheshire, was that if I wanted to get on in the world I needed to lose my 'Manchista' (sic) accent. So, I did. It's only since living in London that people say they can tell where I come from originally. Of course regional accents are rather more acceptable these days.

If you've read this far, you may have realised that I have been influenced through my life by those who I've admired. I've mentioned parents, early bosses, early friends, although I haven't yet mentioned my mate John, who taught me about girls but that's another story. We learn from the patterns we recognise, from the people we admire and from the stories we hear. My aim with this book is to reproduce some of the stories, some of the anecdotes, some of the simple case studies where I and hopefully readers can learn some of the secrets of success.

One thing my professional training taught me was the benefit of continuous learning. I experienced this in broking with the introduction of exams by the Stock Exchange and later the regulators; by being a member of ICAEW (the Institute of Chartered Accountants in England and Wales); and by being an accredited member of the Association for Coaching. The concept of CPD – continual professional development – has shown me how relevant and important it is to keep oneself on the upward curve, continually keeping up to date with modern methods, modern ideas and innovative solutions. The peer groups also espouse this ideal with top-class speaker workshops on every subject imaginable, relevant to successful business leadership and management.

As you can tell, if you've flipped through this book or looked at the beginning of each chapter, there's a poem based on the concepts of each chapter. One previewer told me that as a result of reading all those opening chapters she was able to fully understand what I was trying to communicate when discussing the overall concept. Each of those poems was written as a solid piece of work as soon as I had decided what the overall theme of the book was to be and what the basic content of each chapter was to describe. In other words, I used the poems as an ancillary 'mind map' and mind maps are a terrific way to create a picture of what one is trying to achieve. Fortunately one doesn't need to be an artist to create mind maps, just large sheets of paper and coloured pens or a relatively simple and often free bit of software.

Success

I have been asked
What **success**
Means to me;
Success where?
In life
In business
In love
In wealth
In abundance
In poetry
In prose
In London
In the world
It's all these things
It's all these places
Time changes feelings
Time rewards patience
Reaching out
Into the bright sunlit landscapes
Of the world
And of the mind
Success is performing
Live on a big stage
In the centre of
An arena
In the centre of a bowl
Performing the
Longings of a life
Developed and assured
Living and loving
Amongst the peers
And the giants

Of this civilization
Speaking eloquently
To an audience
Both active and
Passive
One that wishes
To hear all;
Creative innovators
Lucky to be...
Lucky to be there
In the midst
Of a tumult
Adored
Worshipped
Admired
Revered
Followed
Praised
Loved
Respected
Agreed with
Transported to a Heaven
On earth;
That is
Success
To me.
You decide
What
Success
Means to
You.

CHAPTER ONE

Success

Background to success – my early career.
What it means to achieve success; business is not a
one-talent show nor is it a linear performance.

SUCCESS FOR me started in stockbroking, helping my clients to be successful investors. This was instilled in me by my boss, David Hunter. He was the grandson of Henry Cooke and while he espoused the then modern methods, he was a member of the 'old school' as were his partners, most of whom eventually became my partners as I grew up in the business. He believed, like Jose Silva (US parapsychologist, 1914–1999): "Success is not for the timid. It is for those who seek guidance, make decisions and take decisive action".

I had got there with the help of a good friend of mine John (now Lord) Lee (of Trafford) who had left the accounting firm, Royce, Peeling, Green & Co where we were both articled clerks to work at Cooke's and was now moving on again to start a private bank. He told me they were looking for 'a Jewish accountant' to help them move forward and to reach into the Jewish community. It is interesting that years later, the firm was 'reaching out' into the Chinese community and I have no doubt that its successor firm Brown Shipley, is well entrenched with other ethnic and cultural groups.

The parallel is with my old school, Manchester Grammar (I was not one of its best scholars), which had a strong Jewish contingent; one of only two boys of Indian extraction was the aforementioned Ben Kingsley, the actor, although that wasn't his name back then. There were no students of Chinese origin and very few other ethnic minorities. How things have changed. It was and still is a great school, 500 years old in 2015, and I still keep in touch being involved with the London section of the old boys' association.

My 'interview' at Cooke's was lunch with the senior partners (we eventually grew the business from old fashioned partnership through unlimited company, to limited company and finally to PLC). Lunch was the key means of getting and creating business relationships, the mutual understanding, which in turn helped create what was voted at one time, 'the UK's favourite stockbroker' by readers of the *Investors Chronicle*. As far as I was concerned, I was told that the only thing I had to show was that I knew the importance of taking the band off my cigar before smoking! Rather different from the recruitment processes of today.

Networking and relationships leading to success

One of the keys to success in business apart from relationships is the process of networking in order to connect with those with whom you wish to relate, which some find quite difficult. To this day, I still find it a challenge entering a room full of people and striking up *ad hoc* conversations. Perhaps it's a result of being told as a child, not to talk to strangers! However, networking then as now, is one of the best ways of building business, all part of the 'relationship' concept that we'll come to later.

The success I mentioned above has been the keystone of everything I've tried to do and tried to instil in my children and clients over the years. I believe success is derived from an understanding of others, an understanding of old and new methods, an understanding of finance and an understanding of creating innovation, of thinking differently and an ability to spot what your customers don't yet know they want.

Ken Robinson, a well-known educationalist and world-class speaker in the top 20 on TED.com, published a wonderful book not long ago, entitled *The Element*. It's about people making the most success by being where they are a natural fit, where they are 'in the zone', where their passion lies.

Regrettably, too many people are unable, unwilling or just ignorant of where they ought to be in life. If that sounds patronising, it's not meant to be. It's just a fact that recognition of this concept can be quite rare, is certainly not acknowledged by our education system and thus, often we don't produce the right people for the right environments. If we did I'm sure that our success as a nation would be even greater than it is – yes, I still think Britain is one of the best places in the world to live and work despite its obvious problems. I hope that by the time my grandchildren reach adulthood that this is still the case.

The poem 'success' spells out what success means to me and for those who believe success is about making shed loads of cash, then please read no further. To me this is not success; it is merely one manifestation of what success could be for some people. Don't get me wrong, I don't have an 'away' driver about money; I just don't believe that it is the only badge of success, although, of course, it is quite useful!

I wasn't a 'performance poet' then, but the acting and the poetry has added a different dimension to my time in business and does, I believe, certainly help me to espouse those characteristics, which I am trying to use to help others achieve success in business and I guess in life too. It's interesting to me to find that the drivers in business are often the things that are going on 'back at the ranch'. The domestic issues with significant others, life partners or whatever you prefer to call them. Concerns with one's children, one's personal finances, one's domestic relationships often take over the daily focus necessary to run the business and sometimes drive us in the wrong direction by influencing us to make the wrong decisions. Another good reason for having a peer group with no agenda other than your own to help you make the better decisions.

Accountant, poet, coach

So, what's all this 'accountant, poet, coach' stuff about? A corporate financier, who has published many books, Jo Haigh, on learning that I'd invented this new three-word strap line for me, asked what she could call herself – after a few moments she came out with 'financier, mother, goddess'. Those who know her will agree that it's not too far from the truth! For me, I wanted to encapsulate my ideals, my experiences, my concerns and express them in such a way as to help others understand what I am, what I stand for and perhaps, how I can help them. Certainly since adding these words to my LinkedIn profile, I have enjoyed a far higher connectivity with people I do, and would like to, work with.

This takes me back to networking and in turn, social media. What a different world we live in now and how useful it is to be able to keep in touch with contacts when they move on. Following careers using Twitter, Facebook and the like is not only interesting, it is also a godsend when trying to tap into the people one knows and can be helpful in a new business or social endeavour. Yes, it is true that some of it can be overwhelming but thankfully there's always the 'delete' button.

Time is the 'issue'

Practically every new and existing client I meet or work with complains about the lack of time. It's everyone's issue including mine. I often refer to the fact that a while ago, in the States, I bought a copy of *The 4-Hour Work Week* by Timothy Ferriss but that I haven't had the time to read it yet!

It's obvious that we all have the same number of hours in the day, week, month, etc. It's how we use them that matters. This is allied very closely to the art of delegation. We've all said or heard say "by the time I've asked X to do the job, I could have done it myself". Sure you could but you'll have to continue doing it yourself, you'll not train your people, which is a travesty, and you'll never reach your goals – again this is part of succession planning that we'll cover in a later chapter. You will realise that the older you get, each hour is a smaller fraction of your life and so it's easy to see why, as time goes on, it seems to go faster and faster. That is one reason my mentor in writing this book, Mindy Gibbins-Klein, the Book Midwife, insists on a straitjacket of 90 to 100 days from start to finish.

Counter influences

So, with whom do I disagree and which of those people have had an influence on my life? I suppose I disagree mostly with politicians, whether of the right or of the left, and not just because I would do it differently. Isn't it interesting how so few successful business people make a success of politics as a career – I guess because, particularly in this country, with its adversarial system, business leaders want to discuss, make a final decision and get on with it. This can't happen in opposition and it is very difficult for it to happen in government. How few business leaders in politics have really made their mark, really made a success and certainly not in universal opinion? However, politicians do make me think, although I have tried not to be influenced in a biased way, trying always to make my own mind up on the important – if not emotive – matters of the day.

Who else irritates me? I have little patience for what have been called 'meanderthals' those who wander through the streets of London (and I suppose elsewhere) blocking footpaths and preventing me and others from making the sort of progress we believe is our right. Some would say they have a right to their pace and trajectory but perhaps they could show a modicum of thought for others. I have long given up stressing about traffic jams. At least one can always phone ahead these days (ever mindful of road safety!) to tell one's counterpart one will be late. I tell everyone that since living in London I'll either be half an hour early or half an hour late! But these are trivial examples.

Just who do I disagree with? I guess I'm fairly easy going and try to find the good points in otherwise erroneous positions. I was married for over forty years and for the latter part of that time probably disagreed with almost everything my wife had to say, even though she is a highly intelligent woman. Is that significant I wonder? Do others suffer from the same syndrome? A friend once told me that he had survived married life with two words, 'yes dear'. I'm afraid that I haven't the capacity to be so passive!

Whatever my views about all these groups and individuals, I can't put my finger on particular examples of situations so I must assume that the overall environmental factors have, in themselves, been an influence. However, I am not a philosopher, I am an accountant (left-brained[1], neat and tidy, calculating, active), a poet (right-brained, instinctive, creative, passive) and a coach (endeavouring to combine left and right brains to ensure whole-brain thinking by both myself and my clients).

---

[1] See page 194 for a note on left brain/right brain research

Multiple attributes

How can I
Have multiple attributes
When
I am only one
Person?
Do I have more than one persona
And thus
Embody
More than one
Attribute?
Indeed
Let us look
At all those things
That make up
The
Multiple
The multiple
Persona
Or should that be

Personae?
No matter,
We live
We work
For a multi-
Sensational society
A multi-sensational
Business environment
And so, a multi-dimensional
Universe;
A universe
Set out
To cater for multi-
Dimensional businesses
Multi-dimensional lives
So, the attributes
Must themselves
Create the multiple.

CHAPTER TWO

Using multiple attributes to drive business success

The prognosis is that to be successful in business, as in life, one needs a number of separate and distinct attributes. It's more than one thing that drives business success.

WHILE WE can't be everything, we do need to combine accountant, poet, coach in our business. So for those who are not that number-oriented, for those who can't rhyme or scan for toffee, for those to whom a coach is something we take for a trip to the ski slopes, how on earth can we manage, lead, let alone build, a business?

If you seriously believe that you don't have all those attributes then you have to collect about you a team of those who have. It has been said in another way; that every new business needs three partners, the technician, the entrepreneur and the financier. For me, it's accountant, poet, coach.

Results come too late

I strongly believe that one must understand the numbers to be successful. I don't mean actually being a qualified accountant but certainly having undergone some training if it doesn't come naturally, some learning about how the numbers run, how to decide what the key results indicators (KRIs) should be, but ever remembering that by the time you get the results it's too late. So, in addition, you need KPIs (key performance indicators).

You need a fool-proof way of knowing how your business is doing and what changes you need to make to ensure that it does better. Having or being a good bookkeeper is not enough. You must understand what the numbers are telling you. If you can't then you must have someone who can help. The best is to be able to look at a budget, to be able to look at a balance sheet, to be able to look at a profit and loss account and be able to see what's missing, to see what's wrong. Being a poet, i.e, using the right-hand side of the brain[2], helps here.

By accountant I mean someone who has financial understanding, has financial acumen, is able to lead the financial debate, can manage the finance team to get the numbers out that tell all not just how the business is doing but how it is likely to do and thus what changes are necessary to people and non-people overheads. Do we need to invest more or cut costs? And, if we do what will be the outcome? Do we have the financial acumen to be able to predict the Return on Investment (ROI) or the result of cutbacks? It is quite useless

---

[2] *See page 194 for a note on the science of left and right brain*

to come to the end of a financial period and even worse to await financial results sometime after that period to realise that something is going wrong. One has seen such in some of the less than successful companies that have come across the bows. By that time it's often just too late.

Am I saying that all accountants or the 'accountant part' of the business leader are merely left-brained? No, but what I am saying is that if they are that way inclined they must learn to open up the right side and think in a broader way, use broader perceptions and focus on the wider and not just the narrower issues. It's all very well knowing how many widgets are in the store, but you also need to know how many should be there, how many could be there and how many you should manufacture for the upcoming season and indeed, that they are the right widgets. Unless the business leader has a grasp of this, how on earth are they going to run and develop the business to success?

So, what are the financial drivers? Clearly sales lead the way forward but how many and why that many? We have all seen the 'dream sheets' which purport to forecast wonderful sales figures and thus magical profits and – here's the irony – as I said, my prognosis is that every business needs accountant, poet, coach and who is the better dreamer? The poet, of course! But the accountant must embody the poet in order to be able to be creative, in order to be able to be innovative, in order to be able to forecast just where the company will succeed in its selling effort.

This book is not intended to be a sales primer nor is it intended to be a training manual for business leaders. It is aiming to put forward the idea that in order to be successful, businesses need a combination of attributes, a melange of contradictions in many ways, so that it can embody all the difficulties of the growing entity. Too many people set up in business because they want to deliver a product or service that appeals to them but, again, as reported in *The E-Myth*, the structure of the business needs to be built so that it embodies all the individual and separate skills and traits necessary. In the beginning most, if not all, will have to be provided by one or two people.

Delphine Arnaud, daughter of the founder of luxury goods empire LVMH Bernard Arnaud, and now executive vice-president, who was recently interviewed by the FT, says, "It is really very difficult to manage a company and at the same time be very creative. I find that it is our responsibility as leaders of a group to help them... The biggest problem facing young designers is they have treasury problems, they have to pay for the fabrics, and then make productions, and pay for things wholesale. They are trained to create but they don't learn business at school, so it's difficult. And they are very small companies so they can't hire people – they have to manage their own sales, collections and to create".

How on earth is this possible? Seek help, learn, take advice; why make the mistakes that others have made before you? But, doesn't advice cost money? Sure, barter! Swap ideas, product, concepts. Financial and other arrangements can, and should, be made. Recommend others to others and reciprocate. If you can't just swap, set up a triangle where A recommends B, B recommends C and C recommends A. Some very successful businesses have been developed in this way. If that's not poetic don't worry, at least it's a balanced and rhythmic process!

There are any number of business groups, where people at the embryo stage and later can get together for just this purpose. Often they are 'breakfast groups' that meet at an unearthly hour but they all have the one thing in common that every business, new or established, must have, that is, process. A rigid process that is adhered to, and where the 'boss' is held accountable by more than themselves.

Process and patterns

This leads neatly on to the concept of process, which, in itself is the voice of the accountant and in this context we're not just talking about the numbers. Process, is of itself mathematical. It is a series of counting projects, a series of patterns developed for the prime purpose of seeing that everything gets done. Readers will be familiar with 'the sales process' where an estimate is made, for example, of contacts to be made, resulting conversions, meetings held and ultimately sales accruing. Such processes can and should be used for almost every other aspect of business. Everything must have a target, a deadline and an expected outcome, which can be used to forecast the resources needed to achieve the desired result. This is the case whether it's recruitment, building relationships, networking, continuous learning and so on; all subjects covered in this book. So, processes – mathematical formulae for success.

I will be eternally grateful to the late Brian Warnes, a well-regarded accountant with a poetic mien. Author of *The Genghis Khan Guide to Business* (long out of print but still available at a hugely inflated price from Amazon) and his successor Bob (the builder) Gorton, who majored on process and patterns in business and in particular the concept of 'break-even' – where are you in relation to your break-even point? What can you do to make it more flexible whether it's by price increases, by sales increases or by lowering overheads – in fact those are the only three processes you can undertake to make such change.

Turnover	10,000*	11,000	10,000	10,000	This can be either actual or forecast; Increasing turnover will improve breakeven percentage
Margin	40%*	40%	45%	40%	Increasing percentage margin will improve breakeven percentage
Sales cost	6,000	6,600	5,500	6,000	
Margin £	4,000	4,400	4,500	4,000	
Overheads	3,000	3,000	3,000	2,750	Reducing indirect costs will improve breakeven percentage
Profit	1,000	1,400	1,500	1,250	
B/even %	75.00	68.18	66.67	68.75	This figure needs to be no more than 80% otherwise it's a danger signal

In this model only change the starred* items
Work out breakeven by dividing fixed overheads by margin and express as a percentage.
Thus in this model £3,000/£4,000 = 75%

Brian always began his workshops by demonstrating patterns, showing how during the Cold War the US laughed at random splashdowns around the Pacific Ocean thinking that the Russians could not get their warheads to land in the same place. Then someone overlaid those splashdowns with a map of the USA and showed it was taking out four key nuclear command posts, the location of one of which they thought was secret. He applied this concept of spotting patterns to business with great effect.

We learn that in life we make our way forward by recognising patterns and by making decisions based on the patterns we experience; so it has to be in business but I wonder how many people just do things as a result of past patterns without realising that is what they are doing. So, to succeed we must make our own patterns by creating and following a process.

So, how do we create such a process? From what I've just said, it is clear that we should avoid being fixated by our previous patterning or learned behaviours. It is, in my view, essential that we develop our processes by thinking differently, by using the whole brain and not just half of it.

The poet

The point here is that we must exercise our 'poet', to be creative, be imaginative, be dynamic and above all be succinct. We've all seen far too many business plans that go on for ever and are quite meaningless. As mentioned earlier, Robert Frost said that, "poetry takes life by the throat". So it does and so it can in business. I don't mean that the business leader should be sitting in their office writing rhyming couplets. What I do mean is that they should let their mind wander over all the possibilities, let themselves, as Nancy Kline puts it, have "time to think".

We discuss later the fact that TS Eliot had been an investment banker, Paul Gauguin a stockbroker; Damien Hirst, the artist, is also one of the most creative and successful businessman of recent times, someone who has proven that artists need not be dead before their work becomes of monetary value. (Although clearly some of his subjects are in that condition before the process of formaldehyde is effected!)

It's that idea of creating ideas, of innovating, of being different, of dreaming up new ideas before our customers know they want them. After all no one said they wanted a phone that took photographs before the first smartphone was developed. It has often been quoted that when Disney did their market research into family entertainment, no one came up with Disneyland. Henry Ford said you can have any colour so long as it's black and everyone accepted that until someone else produced a red car. Then again, it was Ford who said, "if you believe you can, if you believe you can't, you're right." So too in business. Believe that you can be that poet in your business, be the dreamer as well as the executioner.

There is a danger that in applying this concept, we become too literal but it is not entirely metaphorical. It has long been thought that the right side of the brain is scientifically shown to be the more creative and less linear side. I feel that it is true that those who are more right-brain oriented (but see later for a note on more recent brain research) also use the left side for rationality; but it is also a fact that we make most of our decisions by using intuition (right side) and rationalise later. There has even been an advertising campaign by Alfa Romeo showing a beautiful car with no caption except the words 'rationalise later'.

We make one of the biggest decisions in life when we buy a house for a home. We rationalise by asking ourselves about location, price, transport and school facilities and then make the final decision by whether one likes it or not, or indeed, in my case, whether my wife liked it or not. George Bernard Shaw said, "Reasonable (rational) people adapt themselves to the world. Unreasonable people attempt to adapt the world to themselves. All progress, therefore, depends on unreasonable people."

Earlier in this chapter, we talked about the numbers; we're now talking about the words. The use of words is as important in business as the use of numbers, be it advertising slogans, blogging, even writing emails and SMS messages! The use of the 'poetic' in the sense of putting the words together, not just to be logical but to get our meaning across, to get our product sold, to encourage and motivate our workforce, to present to potential customers. Hopefully we don't bore them with endless PowerPoint slides with bullet points when seven words or a picture or video would create a much more powerful message.

We are very lucky today that we have such amazing technology that we can even make such a presentation with little more than a pocket projector and smartphone. To me this is poetry. I remember years ago being asked to give a lecture on financial services at the Manchester Metropolitan University, a reincarnation of what had been, since its foundation, the Manchester College of Commerce. I had my acetate slides that I'd painstakingly hand drawn the night before and was all set to speak so pressed the switch on the overhead projector only for the bulb to blow. Union rules meant that I couldn't continue until a technician had been found. The students had to talk among themselves for half an hour, so to this day, slide shows are something I avoid like the plague. Talk about patterning!

Numbers plus words plus questions

So, who or what puts the numbers and words together? That has to be the coach. Be it a sports coach, a life coach or a business coach – all help the individual drive towards success. We need to remember that the swimmer Mark Spitz, who won eight gold medals at the Munich Olympics in 1972, had a coach who couldn't swim. The best golfers have a number of coaches all focused on one particular aspect of the game, be it putting, driving, the swing, etc. The business coach is no different. This is someone who is able to look at the business from the outside, who is able to ask the difficult questions, who has not 'gone native' on what is trying to be achieved. Whether a business person employs such a coach is not the point, they have to be their own coach. They have to be able to stand outside and, as it were, examine the swing, see what's going right and what's going wrong. Not only must they be their own coach, they must also learn, as leader, to be their managers' coach. Is this possible? I believe that it is. The concept of 'servant leader' has been around for a long time; this is no different.

Coaching models

The 'boss', to be able to grow the business, has to understand the various coaching models in order to help the team understand where they're going, the targets they need to aim for. One system is the CIGAR model of coaching.

CIGAR

C Current situation

I Ideal situation

G Gaps *(between current and ideal)*

A Actions *(To be taken)*

R Review

There is also, the 'GROW' model, slightly better known.

GROW

G Goal

R *(current)* Reality

O Options *(or obstacles)*

W Way forward

There is a huge amount of information about these and many others on the net that we can call upon, but it should suffice to recall these two in order to make the point.

Balanced scorecard

Another way of looking at the business would be to consider the Kaplan and Norton balanced scorecard model (see Chapter 7 page 105). This is where the business combines a review with focus on several different aspects of the business, its customers, its internal processes, its training and development, all leading to the results. So, as I've said before, by the time you get the results, it's too late; the process by which you get there is all important. There have been many developments on the original concept, not least by the original authors, although there is some doubt as to whether they were indeed the originators. It's just that their book published in 1992 was the most popular.

The boss as coach not only needs to set the vision, they need to help set the values to be espoused by the team. Only by asking questions, by acting as coach, can this be achieved. Let us look at this rationally: everyone we come across will have a different set of values. Many of these stem from the patterning referred to earlier, the patterns learnt when growing up, the patterns learnt from the community, the patterns learnt from their educators. Thus their values have become ingrained. It is difficult to change those inherent values. However, it is necessary that they be aligned, not just with those laid down by the business leader who will, of course, have their own, but also with the values of customers, suppliers and all stakeholders including owners, who may or may not be the same as the business leader in post. It is, however, likely that an owner will indeed share the values of the leader they have put in place to look after their interests or, who the leader has been keen to select as a source of capital to develop and enhance the business as it grows.

The process of ensuring that there is an alignment of values can be complex. It is not a case of changing attitudes but ensuring that everyone involved fully understands each and every separate value system espoused by all those to whom we refer. A coach, or leader as coach, can help bring all this together but it can be a long process to create that understanding.

In order to ensure that not only values are aligned, but that there is the focus on vision and targets we talked about, we again need a process. One of the best tools I have come across is the one-page business plan by Kraig Kramers (who at the time of writing has unfortunately just died) in his book *CEO Tools*, which gives a really helpful example of this. It covers the business planning and execution from start to finish; from vision, through mission (also known as 'customer purpose'). Put simply, vision is the business as perceived by those in it and mission, the business as perceived by its customers. Competitive advantage, which we used to call USP or Unique Selling Proposition, is next. Some say this now needs to be ESP or Emotional Selling Proposition.

Your company name
Business Plan Name

1-Page Business Plan[1]

Vision. *Describe the business we will build (in a few well-constructed sentences).*

Mission Statement. *Describe the purpose, focusing on benefits for the customer.*

Competitive Advantage: *Use numbers that can be authenticated*

Objectives. *First, sales; second, profitability; no more than 6-8 "SMART" objectives: specific, measurable, action-oriented, include results, time-delimited.*

-
-
-
-
-
-
-

Strategies. *Statements that set direction, philosophy, values and methodology for building the business and managing the enterprise. Use 4-6 core strategies common to the industry.*

-
-
-
-
-
-
-

Plans. *Business-building or infrastructure-building action steps necessary to implement the overall plan. Include completion date.*

---

[1] *Adapted from CEO Tools by Kraig Kramers*

Customer purpose (mission)

What makes the customer want to buy from us? If we can really understand that and we can help the customer to really understand the benefits in such a way as they just do, then it is likely that they will not only want to buy from us they will feel that they absolutely need to buy from us. My belief is that this is taking the concept of wants and needs, features and benefits, to a much higher level than ever before. This is especially necessary now that the internet has turned the marketing model on its head. We can no longer broadcast to our potential customers, we have to magnetically draw them in and once drawn in we have to ensure that the poles are in alignment.

Once we understand why we're in business and our customer understands why we're in business, we can move on to our strategic thinking process and develop the strategy needed to move towards our vision. Once we have the strategy we can work on the objectives and once those are defined, our tactical plans can be developed. Once again we must have a thorough process requiring numbers, words and questions, all used and all of benefit.

Cash

Yes, we will need specialists in the business as it grows but there needs to be that initial balance of accountant, poet and coach. Without it, there is a huge danger that cash will run out. It has often been said that "cash is king". Nothing could be truer. Without cash, the business lubricant, how do we pay the wages, order raw materials, pay the rent? How many businesses have we seen where profit is being made only to find it has no cash to pay the taxes, the very reason PAYE was invented[3]? So, how do we ensure that there is always sufficient cash? This is where wishful thinking doesn't work! This emphasises the need for a process; we need not only a means to generate, but also to collect and to count. The process of assessing break-even described earlier, which is predicated on margin (i.e. gross margin, the difference between sales revenue and cost of sales and then working out the fixed overheads of the business and seeing how much cover there is of that margin over the fixed overheads), will enable us to apply both our rational and creative brains to anticipate and to manipulate our cash results.

A very useful exercise is to calculate just how many months' overhead a business has represented by its accumulated cash, its cash at bank or, at least, its bank facilities. Dependent on the nature of the business and in particular how many times a year creditors and debtors are turned over, the business will be able to see and hopefully to adjust accordingly. Too much cash can be as bad as too little. A little 'poetic' evaluation may be helpful here! It's a pity that what my dad used to call debt is now called credit!

So where does this take us? Have we seen why it is absolutely essential to identify the elements we talked about? A look at some of the greatest business books published will confirm that what we have said is on the right track. Perhaps it is Jim Collins and his seminal work, *Good to Great*. The concept there as some readers will remember is that business development is like trying to move and create eventual momentum with a giant iron flywheel. The hedgehog principle described in that book asks: what drives our economic engine? What are we most passionate about? What can we be best in the world at? These all add up to the flywheel driver. In my view they also add up and are equivalent to the influence of the accountant, the poet, and the coach.

Get a Grip by Wickman and Paton – when assessing employees, "does he get it, does he want it, is he capable of doing it?" – is clearly another way of identifying the same concept. *The Element*, Ken Robinson's work mentioned in Chapter 1, puts it rather differently, espousing the concept that people need to be where they naturally fit to ensure their own success – the poet encapsulating the accountant and the coach does this admirably.

So, what is all this telling us? What are the lessons to be learned? Have all business leaders got it in their physiology to be all three – accountant, poet, coach. Not necessarily, but all have the ability to ensure that the three attributes are considered, espoused, developed and recruited in order to make it possible for their business to be successful, for the entity to grow, to prosper, to blossom into the fully grown and beautiful tree of which they, their team and their connections can all be admiring and proud. Society needs successful businesses in order for there to be an environment which can be enjoyed by all, rich and poor. Business not only brings employment, it brings entertainment, it brings education, it brings a benign counterbalance to all the problems and issues that we read about on a daily basis, whether here or abroad. Business not

---

[3] *Pay As You Earn, the system used in the UK to ensure that cash deducted at source from payroll is sent immediately to HMRC (IRS).*

only provides the wherewithal for happiness and success, it brings a platform of joy and contentment supporting the arts, supporting sport and leisure, supporting the state and thus making for a fully rounded, multi-cultural, multi-sensational society.

The financial drivers, the language drivers and the questioning, all separate and all together, work hard at producing the results needed for success. We can analyse results but, as has been said, by the time we see results it's too late so we need to ensure that in driving forwards those results are the right ones for the business. How do we know? We have set a vision and we have set targets but do they feel right, do they jump out at us with a certain resonance that we 'know' deep down that it's all going to work? What we have to do is ask the right questions. How do we know what are the right questions? By allowing the conscious and the unconscious minds to rove over the analysis, to assess by instinct as well as by use of the fine-toothed comb. It needs a combination of all to give us that feeling of "yes, it's right!", "yes, we've done what we set out to do!", of "yes, we knew all along!".

What a great feeling at the end, but once more, the prognosis is that by using the multiple attributes, we just 'know'.

Multiple Perspectives, Multiple Perceptions

As we will see
At a later
Point, we need
To combine
Our perspectives
But first, we need
To be eloquent
In our
Understanding
Of each and every single
One
Of those
Many
Diverse
And separate and
Ultimately and
Necessarily
Separate issues

So that we
Can
Understand
The objectives
The targets
The vision of
Success,
Always
Returning to that
One clear and
Unequivocal goal
The vision
We wish
To reach
In the allotted
Time
With the allotted energy
Of life, in business

CHAPTER THREE

Benefitting from multiple perspectives, multiple perceptions

It's not 'one size fits all'.

Perspective, noun:

1. The art of representing...
2. A particular point of view
3. Understanding of the relative importance of things.

Perception, noun:

1. The ability to see, hear, or become aware of something through the senses
2. The process of perceiving something
3. A way of understanding or interpreting something
4. Intuitive understanding; insight

Compact Oxford English Dictionary, Third Edition, revised 2008, revised & reprinted 2012.

In planning this book, the study of business and the various different aspects thereof, I have oscillated between calling this chapter 'Multiple Perspectives' or 'Multiple Perceptions'. Two very similar words with sometimes quite different meanings if not import. I have therefore persuaded myself to combine the two.

We always need to look at things differently and to consider things from different points of view. This is particularly the case in business, whether we have really nailed the vision or not. This may seem a dialectic considering my comments in the previous chapter but, hopefully, it will become clearer as this chapter develops.

I have stated the view that all businesses need a triumvirate of accountant, poet and coach, be that in one person or in a team. The accountant, numerate and ordered; the poet, literate and rhythmical; the coach, asking difficult (or stupid) questions. So, needed separately and jointly, interacting with each other, using the multiple perspective (point of view) and the multiple perception (understanding) to drive the business forward.

A business, in order to reach its stated vision, needs a rhythm, needs a process, and needs an impetus to push forward towards success. It also needs to see things from different points of view, from that of all its stakeholders and to understand the attitudes of those stakeholders, in order to be able to interact and relate successfully with them.

Stakeholders

So, who are the stakeholders? They are a multitude of interested parties, far more than we sometimes appreciate. In order to progress we need to understand and allow for their perspectives, their perceptions.

Just for the record, here is a list of all those who could be interested in your business:

* *Shareholders*
* *Bankers and other lenders*
* *Other investors*
* *Creditors*
* *Debtors*
* *'C' suite – senior management*
* *Staff – support, e.g. finance, HR, learning and development, technical*
* *The operating team – sales, marketing, production*
* *Customers – wholesale, retail*
* *Suppliers – goods, services*
* *Families of the team*
* *HMRC – Corporation tax, VAT, PAYE, National Insurance, personal tax*
* *Professional advisers – accountants, lawyers, surveyors, consultants*
* *And finally, as introduced by Company Law, society in general where companies have an obligation to consider society when formulating their plans of action, although the way some behave you would never know!*

This list is not necessarily exhaustive but nevertheless it can be seen that any business, both large and small, has to deal with people who will see the business differently and will have differing attitudes towards it. In many of these cases those inside will have to differentiate the completely distinct circumstances, needs and wants and accommodate accordingly.

Black Swans and the unexpected

What about the 'Black Swans', those events that, according to Nassim Nicholas Taleb, just come from left field, are totally unexpected and can disturb equilibrium however carefully it has been crafted? So, the expected and the unexpected have to be taken into account – the 'known unknowns' and the 'unknown unknowns' to paraphrase a former US vice-president, Donald Rumsfeld. Interesting that the press tore him to pieces over this, but with hindsight there was huge wisdom in what he had to say. The full gamut of this model is:

Known unknowns	**Known knowns**
Unknown unknowns	**Unknown knowns**

Known knowns, unknown knowns, unknown unknowns and known unknowns! In other words, the things we know we know and the things we don't know that we know and then the things we don't know that we don't know and the things we know we don't know. A very valuable exercise in perception is to enumerate these four categories in a business. It will help you understand and perhaps even anticipate what might happen, whether it be by disruptive marketing or new legislation – particularly in regulated businesses but even in so-called non-regulated businesses we have the regulations pertaining to, *inter alia,* employment, taxation, importing, transport and so forth.

Rhythm in business 1

So, numbers, words, questions, together provide a rhythm in business, be it the balanced scorecard, the poetry of numbers, or the joy of eloquence intermingled with such concepts as Fibonacci, where nature embodies structural patterns according to an ancient formula which holds true today. The Fibonacci ratio, of 1 to 1.618, otherwise known as the golden mean, rules many aspects of our universe, be it the structure of plants and sea creatures or the ideal (to the human eye) proportions of buildings. As ever, we can see the beauty in numbers in life, in nature. As an aside one might bring in another meaning for the word perspective at this point. These can and perhaps should have a direct influence on the way we conduct our businesses today even though they were discovered and first enumerated in the 13th century by Leonardo Bonacci (c. 1170–c. 1250), known as Fibonacci. This is the Fibonacci spiral.

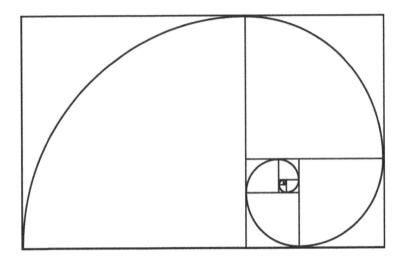

Other structural phenomen include Pi, 22/7, (3.14159265359...) one of the most irregular fractions but one which has such huge ramifications for life and business. A schoolboy mnemonic goes as follows:

Sir, I send a rhyme excelling
In sacred truth and rigid spelling
Numerical sprites elucidate
For me the lexicon's full weight
If nature gain, who can complain
Nor Dr Johnson fulminate.

The number of letters in each word represents the next digit in the series, which seems to go on forever. I understand that no computer has managed to come to a conclusion on this matter although David Thomas, international speaker extraordinaire, has memorised Pi to 22,500 digits. Of course, you can now find Pi to a million characters on the net.

Again the reader will no doubt be questioning what this has to do with business, in the same way that people who leave school and go into employment wonder at the value of having learned the arcane skills of algebra, Latin and the Archimedes Principle! The nature of an education system ought to be to bring out ('educare') the innate knowledge of our children and grandchildren. The fact that they have 'learnt' all this 'stuff' will hopefully mean that they will be able to think things through, to naturally understand, to be able to solve problems and design processes to take companies towards their vision and thus their goals.

So when we put all these natural systems together, recall our experiences and learn to understand all those systems and relate them to where we are and where we are heading, we should be in a position to run businesses, to recruit and employ teams, to develop new products, services and markets and push forward on the journey to success.

When we talk about rhythm in business to what do we refer? Rhythm by its very nature is a regular pattern of happenings, manifestations and characteristics that we can recognise as a vibrant pattern, a veritable snowstorm, where the individual highly patterned flakes come together to provide a blanket, an overlay, which helps the team drive the business forward. It is an understanding of all the individual characteristics that combine to make it work.

To help understand that pattern, it is helpful to have a group of people working together who understand each other, each other's values and where each other is coming from and going to. Hence the need to train them in that eloquence of understanding, admittedly not an easy thing to do but who said leading and managing a business, particularly a growing business, was an easy thing to do?

How do we ensure that there is a rhythm that all can feel, accommodate and recognise? By a cohesive resonance with the overall concept of accountant, poet and coach; by a continuous tension and relaxation of the relationship and interaction between the three. The numbers may be the result of a mechanical process; the words too, can also be made up by design but inevitably that is more difficult, hence the need for the coach to tease out the correct words, the meaningful and the words to which the several parties to the endeavours can relate. This is vital if, as we said in this chapter's poem, we can do things both separately and in combination, always keeping the ultimate goal in sight.

Clarity of presentation

Our people must learn to be more eloquent. How often in business do we have to sit through interminable PowerPoint slides with endless bullet points telling us virtually nothing, or at most, nothing we haven't heard before and would dearly love not to hear again. Teams must be trained properly how to make presentations, be they presentations to colleagues or to customers. The fewer words the better – not for a minute suggesting that the next sales meeting be conducted in verse but the concept of verse where complex issues are covered by a very few well-chosen words, succinctly put, will have much more power than the verbose list of bullet points or, worse still, when whole sentences are flashed to an audience that just does not have the ability to watch a speaker, listen to their words and watch and absorb what is on a screen all in one simultaneous action.

I wish that I had a pound for every executive that I have recommended go to Toastmasters[4] to learn and practice the skills of public speaking. As the master, Dale Carnegie (USA, 1888–1955) said, "you can't have private lessons in public speaking". You need an audience. In Toastmaster meetings it is not only the process of making a series of prepared speeches and being publicly evaluated but also an opportunity to speak off the cuff, something that people in business need to do all the time but very rarely learn to do in a professional way.

So the eloquence of numbers, the eloquence of words and the combination when used expressively can enhance the chances of success in business as in life. An interesting aside could be that what drives business success also drives life success, be that in terms of financial freedom to learn, to travel, to relate and just to enjoy. Again, by combining the processes, we can enjoy the arts, theatre, performances of many types; as we know, sports not just in terms of results, are a combination of statistics which are being used more and more scientifically to drive success than hitherto. As technology develops – in particular wearable technology – we will see considerably more examples of this phenomenon in everyday use.

One wonders why current debate, which has a tendency to focus on the here and now (not to conflict with Eckhart Tolle's concept in *The Power of Now*), doesn't spend a little more energy on looking forward a few – and probably only

4 *www.toastmasters.org*

a few – years, when technology will be solving many of our existing problems. Just to take a simple example to illustrate the point: we have a huge debate on aircraft noise and the expansion of airports. By the time such extensions are built having expended huge amounts of time and money, aircraft will inevitably be quieter than they are now. At least we at last seem to be applying some effort in reducing pollution and reducing the effects of climate change but the balance between current needs and current wants seems to be wholly out of kilter.

Looking at things differently

So, how do we look at things differently in business? How do we think strategically? There are a number of tools and techniques that can be applied. We've all come across the so-called brainstorm where the team gets together to shout out things that could be done, regardless of how strange, difficult or apparently ridiculous they seem. Unfortunately, the next part of the exercise is often done badly rendering the whole thing pointless. What should happen is that the facilitator (and it's always better to have an outsider do this so as not to be 'native' to the process) should encourage the deletion of those ideas that clearly are irrelevant or nonsensical. We then have a long list of things that could be done but are they things that will work towards our vision or are they just 'good ideas'? It is essential to have the endgame in view otherwise the whole exercise becomes a waste of time. How often has the team gone back to base, someone types up the results and that's the last they are heard of? Much, much, better if the process is taken a stage further and a system such as the Six Thinking Hats of Edward de Bono is applied.

This is a process that can valuably be used for any team analysis or even individual analysis. The concept is to split the thinking into half a dozen separate categories. First comes the White Hat signifying the facts and information as known; next the Red Hat, signifying feelings, what we feel about the facts; then comes Yellow to represent the benefits of a course of action or strategy; then Black, the negatives; the thinker(s) then puts on the Green hat – some teams have been known to do this literally – to allow creativity to be brought on stream; finally, the Blue Hat as a check on process, to see that the strict categorisation has been followed. Thus a fully analysed examination of the ideas thrown up in the brainstorm has been undertaken with the result that sensible decisions can be made as to the way forward.

Incidentally, for a while, misplaced political correctness prevented the term 'brainstorm' being used, the suggestion being that epilepsy sufferers would be offended until the Epilepsy Society debunked that idea by conducting a survey of sufferers in 2005!

Group coaching

Coaching models have been referred to in Chapter 2. These models too can be used in the team context. The facilitator/coach will lead the team through a series of stages to reach a conclusion as to the way forward. For example, using the CIGAR model before the brainstorm. The team looks at the overall issue from an inclusive perspective. It decides where it is now (Current) and where it wants to get to (Ideal); it then looks at the Gaps and subsequently works out the Actions it needs to take to get to where it needs to go. The R is the review process where the team checks that its thinking is congruent with the objective. I am always reminded of Alice in *Through the Looking Glass*, one of my favourite books. Our heroine reaches a cross roads and doesn't know which way to go. Looking up she sees the Cheshire Cat grinning in the tree. "Please sir, which way shall I go?" "Where do you want to get to?" asks the cat. "I don't really mind", says Alice. "Well, then, it doesn't really matter which way you go." How many businesses and particularly business meetings are conducted with the same ethos?

One peer group member did, however, recognise the corollary to this concept; we'll call him David, because that's his name. He had started a business developing some very sophisticated communications technology. He referred to himself as 'the best software engineer in the world'. We all assumed that was a bit of hyperbole! Anyway, having shown us some of the things he had produced he admitted that he hated running the business; he just wanted to design and build stuff. So he set about selling his company to an American he knew well, based near Seattle, and became CTO (Chief Technology Officer), while still remaining in Guildford, Surrey!

Another member, around the same time – we'll call him Leonard, although unlike David, that's not his real name for reasons that will become clear – was managing director of a consultancy business working with some very upmarket clients and decided to have an affair with his business partner. This went on for a couple of years until the partner's husband kicked up such a fuss that Leonard went back to his wife and children and sold out of the business. His thinking was not in accordance with a proper business process but it achieved the desired and necessary result!

Business clients come for help, employees are recruited for their skills but human beings turn up and it is thus absolutely essential that business recognises that fact. The old command and control ethos of Victorian times does not work for any number of reasons. Even the armed services, where it is essential to obey orders, recognise that there must be both a logical and a 'felt' list of objectives. In war zones as well as in training arenas, it is a given that the whole person is to be acknowledged otherwise things just do not work. So, in sport or indeed in any business or non-business endeavour, the same applies. Some will inevitably argue with this viewpoint signalling that in matters of the heart we can't just have a cold, logical and unequivocal process. Agreed, that's just the point I'm making. In feeling matters there must be some left-brain thinking and in logical business scenarios there must be right-brain creative thinking. In all scenarios there is a coach/trainer; it might not be a third person but who, in love, doesn't share their thoughts and feelings with a best friend? The parallel need is in business or, indeed, it ought to be.

Can we espouse these thoughts; are we able to employ the techniques needed to create great businesses? Both Buddha and Henry Ford said that we are what we think so let's think that we can and 'just do it' as a well-known slogan has it. I disagree strongly with those who now say that we can't be the best we can. It's not just about thinking positive thoughts although it does help and I've been present in an audience where just one person thinking negatively has changed the whole atmosphere and I've seen that proven scientifically by both Tony Robbins[5] and Nigel Risner[6], two motivational speakers on the circuit.

Finding the better way

Having clear and unequivocal goals where we can see the outcome we are aiming for is only a part of the overall strategy but they play a key role in that strategy and without them, we'll never achieve what we either want or need to achieve. We should go further by having well-thought-out and written goals – and that applies in life generally and not just in business.

'Edward Bear', the formal name for Winnie-the-Pooh, was being dragged down the stairs backwards, "bumpety bump" and thought there must be a better way! Have you found the better way to run your business or do you just believe that there must be a better way?

The challenge is, of course, to find that better way. We've discussed several ways of searching in this chapter. There are many more but one of the most powerful is that of Unlocking Creativity™(See Chapter 12), where the precise use of poetry helps clarify the thinking process and can change cultures and values and has also been known to change lives.

A key part of perception is how the members of the team perceive each other and how well they understand each other.

---

[5]*Motivational speaker, author of* Unleash the Power Within.
[6]*Motivational Speaker, author of* You Had Me at Hello, *on networking.*

We referred earlier to the idea that not all stakeholders hold the same values; this extends to team members. Indeed, it is necessary to build a team where there are different skills, attributes and traits; so how do we ensure that the team understands each other well enough to be able to work together successfully and achieve the necessary results?

The start of that process could be an evaluation, a team appraisal, where not only the team members take part in an exercise but also line managers and subordinates. All answer the same questions as the team itself. A simple questionnaire 'Executive Team Profile' containing 25 questions, each requiring merely a yes/no response is reproduced at the end of this chapter. You can see that if each and every member of the team and those to whom they relate complete this document there will be a much greater understanding of where they are all coming from. The questionnaire just works and easily forms the basis for greater understanding of themselves and of each other. The mere exercise of self-assessment married to peer and other internal voices has been shown to produce remarkable results, proving that perceptions can be changed by the use of different perspectives. Note that each of the captions is a positive statement, only modified by a simple yes or no.

Of course, it is important that everyone plays full out and is honest but when we bear in mind that the process is achieved by everyone being consulted and it is an open process, there should be a huge amount of information shared even if some of it is somewhat negative. It is vital that all perceptions are out in the open to enable a situation of total mutual understanding. With this in place teams will be unable to be dysfunctional and will exhibit a huge level of trust. As Steven M. R. Covey (son of the original Steven R. Covey) in his book *The Speed of Trust* points out, it is trust, particularly in teams, that is the lubricant to help get things done. Indeed, the parallel is that in all areas where there is trust, things happen.

In his seminal book *The Five Dysfunctions of a Team* Patrick Lencioni talks about a hierarchy of dysfunctions: inattention to results, avoidance of accountability, lack of commitment, fear of conflict and ultimately absence of trust. He develops his themes and you immediately notice just how teams will fail if they are not shown how to contribute in such a way as to manifestly adhere to these simple concepts.

So, perception and perspective go hand in hand. We need to look and consider things differently; we need to introduce processes that challenge our thinking so that we can achieve success, if not greatness, through a much greater understanding. To this end, this morning I bought a copy of the *International New York Times* (formerly the *International Herald Tribune*), my favourite holiday reading. It certainly gave me a different perspective on the world than my trusted *Financial Times*.

Executive Team Profile

Directions: For each item, circle Y (for yes) if it describes the person and N (for No) if it does not. Please respond to **every** item for **every** person listed, even though it may be difficult at times. If you feel 60% Yes and 40% No, circle "Yes." Swing one way or another on every item. Write names of team members in the box at the top of each column.

Names	1	2	3	4	5	6
1. Is a good team player	Y N	Y N	Y N	Y N	Y N	Y N
2. Does his/her job competently & skillfully	Y N	Y N	Y N	Y N	Y N	Y N
3. Is a genuinely likable person	Y N	Y N	Y N	Y N	Y N	Y N
4. Good at giving feedback to others	Y N	Y N	Y N	Y N	Y N	Y N
5. Is a good listener	Y N	Y N	Y N	Y N	Y N	Y N
6. Is open and receptive to feedback from others	Y N	Y N	Y N	Y N	Y N	Y N
7. Treats people with dignity and respect	Y N	Y N	Y N	Y N	Y N	Y N
8. Looks for "win-win" solutions to disagreements	Y N	Y N	Y N	Y N	Y N	Y N
9. Good at facing up to tough problems	Y N	Y N	Y N	Y N	Y N	Y N
10. A person you can trust	Y N	Y N	Y N	Y N	Y N	Y N
11. Will "go to bat" for other people	Y N	Y N	Y N	Y N	Y N	Y N
12. Gets along well with almost everybody	Y N	Y N	Y N	Y N	Y N	Y N
13. Uses his/her time efficiently & effectively	Y N	Y N	Y N	Y N	Y N	Y N
14. Will admit it or apologise when wrong	Y N	Y N	Y N	Y N	Y N	Y N
15. Has what it takes to be a good manager	Y N	Y N	Y N	Y N	Y N	Y N
16. Is a good problem-solver	Y N	Y N	Y N	Y N	Y N	Y N
17. Speaks mind, even when it's unpopular	Y N	Y N	Y N	Y N	Y N	Y N
18. Is well-organised	Y N	Y N	Y N	Y N	Y N	Y N
19. Treats people fairly & equitably	Y N	Y N	Y N	Y N	Y N	Y N
20. Good at giving compliments/positive feedback	Y N	Y N	Y N	Y N	Y N	Y N
21. An enjoyable person to be around	Y N	Y N	Y N	Y N	Y N	Y N
22. Open to other peoples' ideas & opinions	Y N	Y N	Y N	Y N	Y N	Y N
23. Is level-headed, even under stress	Y N	Y N	Y N	Y N	Y N	Y N
24. Presents ideas clearly and articulately	Y N	Y N	Y N	Y N	Y N	Y N
25. Has good "people" skills	Y N	Y N	Y N	Y N	Y N	Y N

Definitions

Many years ago
My guru
Told me
Not to be bound
By my own
Definitions.
So what do I mean
By 'definitions'?
The definition of
'Definitions' is... is...
That untouchable, unknowable
Eloquence
Of reason

Of sense
That it works
That it matters
That it
Resolves
The fundamental
Resonances
Risking nothing
And risking everything
In life
In work and,
In business

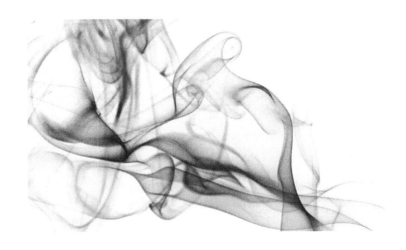

CHAPTER FOUR

Learning the definitions

Accountant, poet, coach and what
they mean for your business.

Definition, noun:

1. A statement of the exact meaning of a word or the nature of or scope of something
2. The action of defining something
3. The degrees of sharpness in outline of an object or image.

In Chapter 2 we talked about multiple attributes, so, what's the difference between that and this section on the definitions? Here it is useful to delve a bit further into the precise nature of what we are talking about, when we use the terms accountant, poet, coach, so let's start with the definitions of these words as laid out in the same dictionary:

Accountant, noun:

A person who keeps or checks financial accounts.

Accountants

What a miserable definition that is. No one trained as an accountant or employed as one would restrict their activity to the above definition. Yet anyone can call themselves an accountant. In the UK and, I have no doubt, elsewhere, it is not a protected word, unlike lawyer, which according to the same dictionary is *"a person who practises or studies law, especially (in the UK) a solicitor or a barrister or (in the USA) an attorney".*

So, how would I, a poet, define an accountant? Well, having trained as one, with five long years of hard study – and it's much harder today than in the 60s! Or at least I'm told it is by those who have embarked on that journey in more recent times. Well, even if, owing to (the lack of) law on the subject, anyone can call themselves an accountant, the description, if not the definition, must be rather more expressive. To me, and for the purpose of this book and my prognosis, an accountant is someone who is learned in the art of finance, is numerate (although not necessarily mathematical) to the extent of being able to add up, recognise patterns and understand what the numbers are telling them. (When I started as an accountant, I would have said 'telling him' but these days more women qualify as accountants than men, although a much smaller proportion become partners in firms!)

That's another thing, becoming a partner in a firm of (chartered) accountants as well as Chartered Certified Accountants – members of a separate professional body – is only one route. Rather more people go into industry, go into business, go into public service and so on than go into practice. Many who stay on the straight and narrow (and by that I mean, retain a link to their training, become financial controllers, finance managers, financial directors, inspectors of taxes, although ironically, many who do gravitate towards a career in HMRC or other parts of public service, are pulled back into professional practice to exercise their skills in becoming creative in the widest sense of that word!). Not too many go into politics unlike their brethren in the legal profession but I suppose that makes sense as politicians are there supposedly to make the law. Accountants, in my view, prefer to interpret the law rather than make it, although, of course, the multitude of lawyers prefers to follow that course as well. But I digress; I ought to be explaining that accountants do not pass caustic comments on the distinctions between them and other professionals.

Accountants are not restricted in what they do to that rather terse definition quoted above. They have a duty and a responsibility to not only gather the numbers together but also to identify, explain, and interpret what the actual numbers are saying and use them, certainly in business if not elsewhere, to help plan, design and manage the business going forward. They need to construct models that help business take the profitable and cash-rich path forward to prosperity and success. That's quite a responsibility but one that should hopefully come naturally to someone who is drawn to the profession from a relatively early age.

The Element was mentioned earlier. It is my view that to be a helpful, dynamic and ultimately useful accountant, the person should have not just ability but an actual flair for the numbers and what those numbers are telling us. The accountant needs to be able to collate, draft, display, interpret and utilise the business numbers in such a way as to help drive forward the ultimate success of that business. In other words, this is not a mechanical responsibility, but one which exhibits an understanding in its self and an ability to help all others in the undertaking to make the best decisions on a day-to-day and longer-term basis. They must not only put the numbers together, they must have the ability to really understand what the numbers are telling them and thus point them and their colleagues forward in the most effective way. This is no mean feat. So, when it comes to recruitment the business owner and leader must know what to look for. In the chapter on recruitment, there is a list of traits that I believe must be inherent in the candidate. As is explained, some of those traits are essential to the effectiveness of the candidate and some are beneficial in selecting the right person for the role. Wooden accountants, those who conform to the dictionary definition, need not apply!

I have a tendency to believe that, in order to fill the bill, if the accountant is to be successful they will need far more skill, passion and drive than could possibly be expected by those who have not thought about the matter in a cohesive and beneficial way. Too many accountants are merely encapsulating the dictionary definition when they need to be much, much more, in order to fulfil the essential job role in the business of the company. Although a serious proportion of chief financial officers (CFOs) in FTSE 100 companies do rise to the CEO role, many lower down the food chain are incapable of so doing merely because they do not have the broad range of attributes needed to help them actually lead the company rather than just support the efforts of senior management and the board. They lack the 'poet'; the ability to think sideways, to think creatively. We're not talking about the euphemism 'creative accountant' here.

Poetry and poets (in business)

We are, however, talking about an ability to work with and/ or embody the characteristics we will now define in 'the poet' and later 'the coach'.

Poet, noun:

1. A person who writes poems (sic!).
2. A person possessing special powers of imagination or expression.

In view of that we should define:

Poem, noun:

A piece of imaginative writing arranged in a particular rhythm and also often in rhyme.

So, once again, it is necessary to further explain what is meant by poet in the business sense. Because the accountant, as described above, has to be served by and serving of numbers, so the poet has be served by and serving of words. So far, simple enough but, in the context of this book and its purpose, we are not talking about someone whose daily task is to write poetry as defined, it is to use words in such a way as to provide powerful and clear messages and also to look inside and to be able to communicate what is going on in the 'creative' side of the brain. To interpret, to explain, to expand and to help expand the minds of the team. Oddly enough it is, in my opinion, necessary for the poet person to do the interpretation of the whole message incorporating the numbers as well as producing the words rather than the accountant. So while the accountant needs the poet, the poet uses the accountant and the accountant's contribution.

The poet also uses intuition in a rather different way because although the accountant needs to interpret the numbers often using intuition so to do, it is the poet who will make understandable the overall message by 'feeling' rather than just by analysis and just by thinking. In order to do this, the poet needs to take time, needs to allow the brain to mull over, cogitate, assimilate and totally consider the output. One of my favourite questions as a coach is "how often do you do absolutely nothing?" The purpose of so doing is to allow the brain to do its own work; the unconscious mind, sometimes referred to as the subconscious, is often hugely powerful when left to its own devices. This is, of course, manifestly obvious when brilliant ideas come to one in the shower, while our consciousness is focused on another entirely different purpose.

I'm not for one moment suggesting that to be effective business people should be taking showers all day long but, as described earlier, the concept of the personal retreat is so valuable as it allows the brain to work without control, without direction. OK, I hear you say, you've no time for all that. That's my challenge to all business people; of course you'd have time if only you would learn to delegate effectively.

As I've said, we all have the same amount of time. Every one of us has the same number of hours in each day. It's how we use those hours that matter. By doing the hard things first and ensuring that they're done, we are then able to do the small and less important things. However, how many of us say to ourselves, "I'll just make these quick phone calls first" and then through interruptions by others we find it's lunchtime before we get down to it? Then we feel that we've no time to actually have lunch or we gobble a sandwich at our desk instead of giving the brain time to think about what we've achieved in the morning. Then, of course, we haven't really achieved anything so the brain starts panicking because it knows the same thing will happen in the afternoon and it'll be tomorrow before we again consider the major project and so it goes on. Mind you, I have just found it easier to write that paragraph than to move on to preparing my annual accounts due in 20 days' time, when I could have done them eight months ago!

Time

Time, noun:

1. The unlimited continued progress of existence and events in the past, present, and future, regarded as a whole
4. The right or appropriate moment to do something
6. The length of time taken to complete an activity

and

11. The rhythmic pattern or tempo (of a piece of music).

There are some wonderful ironies in the selection I've just copied out considering what we've been talking about earlier.

Number 11 applies even more in the context of the poet. So, with all that said, a bit of advice: spend some time working out how you could use your time more effectively, more efficiently, more pleasurably and to greater purpose. Stop being the CFFO, the chief firefighting officer!

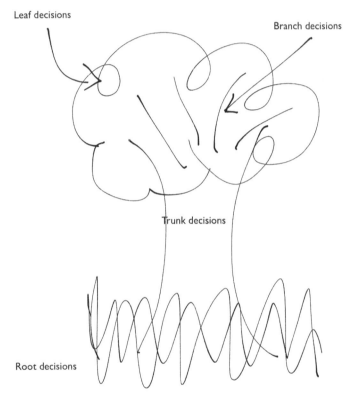

Leaf decisions

Branch decisions

Trunk decisions

Root decisions

The tree (pictured) has four parts. Leaves, branches, trunk and roots. Leaf decisions are for anyone to make; they should just make them and get on with it. Branch decisions are made by your team, action taken and reported back. Trunk decisions are those considered by the team members and discussed with the boss, but with the proviso that the team member should have a preferred course of action in mind and be looking for the go-ahead. Root decisions will be more fundamental and strategic and will possibly need board approval.

So, it can be seen that with a few minutes prior thought we can set up a structure that automatically ensures that much of the leader's time can be saved by endowing the decision-making structure upon the team. What a result!

Well, that was more about time than anything else, but we all know that time is hugely important. As the writer Vivian Greene (UK, 1904–2003, widow of the novelist Graham Greene) said, "Don't wait for the storm to pass, learn to dance in the rain". What a wonderful way of telling us not to procrastinate, not to waste time but to get on with it; that is, whatever we need to get in with rather than what we want to get on with. The difference between 'need' and 'want' is huge. I think most people when they say 'I need a drink' really mean 'I want a drink'!

My old guru, whom I quoted in this chapter's poem, taught me that there are three levels to one's self: 'think, feel and will'. This is ancient philosophy. It is what I'm aiming to reflect in 'accountant, poet, coach'; although not a rigid parallel it is a helpful guide to looking at things 'another way'. The concept is that by using all three aspects of the being, we will achieve far more and achieve far more effective results than only applying the 'think' bit, the 'head' bit, the 'brain' bit. By bringing in at least head and heart, brain and feeling, we make a good start but we really need all three aspects to more than excel. Indeed, excellence, while good, is not really good enough; we need to be outstanding and, as Tony Robbins is fond of saying, being outstanding is just a heartbeat away from excellence. Even Ofsted, the UK's education regulator, uses 'outstanding' as its highest grading when assessing the performance of schools and colleges.

OK, that's the academic and philosophical stuff. What about the practical? As I've said, I don't expect business leaders to be spending their days actually writing poetry. My belief is that poetry can change attitudes, change minds and can raise the mundane to a very much higher plane. We can use it to change cultures, to not only reach difficult goals but to enable us to actually see goals that hitherto we wouldn't have dreamed of – the BHAGs as some call them, the 'big, hairy, audacious goals'. Indeed, to reach such goals it is necessary to aim, as they say, for the stars, that way you have a chance of hitting the moon. Again, everyone in the company needs to be aware of the vision, to be part of achieving that vision. I get concerned when bosses tell me that they can't share their full vision with the team because it's the aim to sell out in due course. Share that with the team by showing them what's in it for them and they'll be alongside and help you achieve your desires. Be like the janitor at Cape Canaveral in the 1950s who was able to say with absolute conviction, when asked what his job was, "I'm helping to put a man on the moon" and of course, by 1960, this was achieved. Much more on vision, its importance and relevance to success, will be found in Chapter 6.

So, why do I believe that the second part of the triumvirate for business success is the poet? Partly because I am one but much more importantly because I firmly believe that if business leaders were to wear the poetic hat, to use poetic exercises (see Chapter 12 on Unlocking Creativity™), to actually write poems, they would be able to switch on the right-hand side, the creative side of the brain and communicate to their teams and stakeholders in a much clearer and more succinct fashion. Furthermore, by teaming up with the accountant and, later, the coach, we will be able to create the right pathways, to follow those pathways and to achieve the necessary vision by so doing.

The way we use words is critical to business. How often do we, whether on the inside of a company or on the outside, read the most pitifully painful and naive statements by those who should know better, who use the most awful clichés, the worst grammar and pretentious sentiments all in the cause of 'motivation'. The obvious irony is that they often create the opposite of motivation by hollow laughter throughout the audience.

The poet – the wordsmith – is able through their skill to interpret, explain, spread the meaning behind the numbers and ensure that the team and others fully understand what those numbers are telling us. It is essential that we don't just read in the numbers what has happened but also what is likely to happen. We need the right words in addition to the right numbers to enable us to fully understand what's going on and what is likely to go on. Equally, in order to market ourselves and sell our products and services, we need to understand and explain the numbers and to express our messages succinctly and clearly at all times.

Rhythm in business 2

As we've said, another aspect of poetry is rhythm. The best companies have a culture that contains a dynamic rhythm. Go into reception, enter the lift and you can palpably feel that rhythm. The staff are clearly part of the fabric of the business, everyone relates positively and dynamically. The visitor feels at home and welcome, the team appear to be on top of their roles even if there are problems – and what business has no problems? If a company leader can set out to ensure that everyone embodies the same values, the same ethos, the same focus on vision then that rhythm should automatically follow. The difficulty is that if it's not there it can be a hellishly difficult journey for all who are involved.

So, how can we be sure that we are focused on the same things, that we are following the same path, the path we want to be on to ensure the success that we're always talking about? Steps one and two are to embody the accountant and the poet; step three is to bring the coach into the equation, so that it truly is 'accountant, poet, coach'.

Coach, noun:

1. An instructor or trainer in sport
2. A teacher who gives private or specialised training.

Regretfully, I have to disagree with these definitions. In the context I wish to use the word 'coach', it is not a trainer, it is not a teacher but, just as I took issue with the word 'education' earlier, a coach is the one who 'brings out' the knowledge of the one being coached. It's all there and needs to be released, to be triggered by a continuing and exhaustive questioning process, one where the person being coached is led through a series of transactions with themselves so that by a process of question and answer that person is enabled to decide for themselves just what needs to be done. It is true that with many coaches, particularly business coaches, an element of mentoring, which is a sort of teaching and training, will enter into the interventions; but in business as elsewhere in life, for success to accrue, the business leader and cohorts who are being coached are the ones to arrive at the necessary actions as a result of the coaching process. If the coachee (horrible word but used all the time in the coaching profession) is told what to do by the coach, who does not necessarily embody the accountant and the poet, they will not be taking the business forward with full knowledge of the business and its whole situation. In saying this I'm trying hard not to differentiate between the internal coach and the external coach (i.e. employed versus consultant).

Companies, in my opinion, need both. The internal coach can be anyone in a line-manager position but for the purpose of this discussion we mean the business leader who must apply their skills, attributes and knowledge in coaching the team. We could call this 'manager as coach'. To be a really good coach and to ask those simultaneously difficult and stupid questions the leader sometimes needs to suspend judgment. I have purposely used the phrase accountant, poet, coach in that order because each word builds on the previous one. The accountant forms the base line; the poet, as explained, takes this forward; and then the coach, by asking those questions, builds on that enhanced foundation and allows things to really happen. Without all three working together, combining their skills, combining their knowledge, there will be a second-rate result.

So really, what is a coach? There are elements of sports coaching in the business world but the parallels can be extended too far. The sports coach has to be very directive; there are times when it is appropriate for the business coach to be directive too but on the whole, it is much better to follow a non-directive course for the reasons explained earlier. What we want is for the manager to work out the best and most effective course of action and not to be told what to do all the time. This neither helps create a devolved operation with everyone knowing what to do and getting on with it nor can anyone feel that ownership of their role.

Workshop speaker, Mark Fritz, poses the question, "why do we never wash a rental car?" Great question and, of course, we know the answer: someone else does it for us because we don't own it. In business if we don't own it, we can't possibly have the same pride in what we do. That's why share options are so valuable because they're endowing the employee with a future share of the business without equity being diluted along the way (the equity holders own the current value but without giving any of that up, they've enabled the team to feel that concept of ownership in a different way).

The coach, by asking difficult questions – a difficult task in itself – is helping the team recognise what they have to do to take the company forward, is helping the team think differently, is helping the team coordinate itself with the longer-term needs of the business and not just with the day-to-day needs, a situation that is absolutely vital if we are to enable the business to grow, to be outstanding. Of course, for a business to be outstanding it needs outstanding people, ideas and resources but how are those obtained? Merely by ensuring a well-thought-out business plan, recruiting the right people and formulating the right strategy. That all needs a combination of accountant, poet and coach.

On the subject of questions, I met a very successful businessman the other day, a South African, who told me that when he was a boy, at his school, prizes were not awarded for those who gave good answers but to those who asked the best questions!

Listening and asking questions

What does it take to be a good coach? Apart from the ability to ask questions, one of the other main attributes is that of being a good listener. How many business people have we met who are not just bad listeners, they seem incapable of listening at all. They are too busy listening to their inner voices to hear and understand what is being said by colleagues and others. They can't wait for the other person to be quiet so that they can express their own opinions. On the other hand, we've all heard that apocryphal Chinese saying that it is better to keep your mouth shut and appear a fool than to open it and let everyone know you are, but we can all think of people to whom this applies too much of the time.

Susan Scott, Seattle author of *Fierce Conversations*[7] says, "Let the silence do the heavy lifting." In other words, by keeping one's mouth shut having asked the basic question, the person being questioned has to think more carefully given the time to answer. The problem is that because 'nature abhors a vacuum' people feel that they've got to answer a question immediately and do so without thinking. So when asking a question, be quiet while you're waiting for the answer and conversely, when asked a question don't immediately rush to answer. By all means say, "that's a good question" but follow it up by saying, "I need a moment to think". Rather than being despised for that, you will be enhanced in the eyes of your interlocutor. Of course, an awful response is, "I hear what you say"; maybe, but are they actually listening?

To return to *Fierce Conversations* for a moment, this is not angry or aggressive conversation, it is about getting to the kernel, getting to the essence. We need to ask the question, "What's the most important thing we should be talking about today?" Yes, by all means, indulge in light chatter in order to learn more about your team and what makes them tick but in one to one sessions where your need is to dig deeper, be really intrusive, push down, ask again and again, "what else?" "What else?" This process is vital in pushing the team forward to the goals that need to be achieved.

Thus, the coach really pushes the accountant and poet to achieve results, to be outstanding, to be beyond good. That is the only way we can achieve greatness in a company, ever remembering that it's the people who are the most important

[7] *See Fierce Conversations by Susan Scott, published in the UK by Piatkus.*

factors in any business. How often have we seen a grade-A product or service fail because we have grade-B people? But on the other hand, grade-A people can often turn around a grade-B product or service.

To conclude this Definitions chapter, as long as we know what we are talking about, what we are defining, we will fully understand the concept of accountant, poet, coach; we will be able to get our act together and move the business forward to that position of outstanding achievement.

Continuous learning

It is
An absolute
Necessity
That we
All continue
To learn
As we go through
Life
And life
In business.
Often, we cannot help
But learn
And learn continuously
However, sometimes
We need to remind
Ourselves
That we must be
Continually

Learning
If only to avoid
Those who would
Aim to disrupt
Our businesses
Disrupt
Our lives
Disrupt
Our profitability
By their cashing in
On our attempts
At success.
So, our endeavours
Must contend
With those others
Who continuously
Learn. Do not
Let them overtake.

CHAPTER FIVE

A process of continuous learning

In running and growing a business
you have to keep learning.

IN THE professional world it's known as CPD or CPE. Continuing Professional Development or Continuing Professional Education. Different professional bodies – and the writer belongs to two such bodies – have different rules and procedures for continuous learning. The idea is that to remain professionally qualified, individuals must keep themselves up to date. The way they do so differs from body to body and, for example, even coaching companies, will lay down rules that their associates and staff members must follow to continue to be eligible to provide those companies' services.

I learned some of these lessons very early on in my career. As mentioned, I trained to be a chartered accountant as what was then called an 'articled clerk'. This was supplemented by a correspondence course of learning produced by a company with the wondrous name of H. Foulkes Lynch. There was a stack of learning to do followed each week by a test to see how much we had remembered. We used to say that the papers were set by Mr Foulkes and marked by Mr Lynch. This, in my case, was followed by a short but intensive course at Lyme Hall near Stockport in Cheshire. When Mary Queen of Scots was being brought south to face trial she was incarcerated in a prison tower in the grounds. It was all very forbidding. Anyway, while passing one's exams with all this help, it was not the end of one's studies. A very few years later, with a young baby at home, I was obliged to sit and pass newly designed Stock Exchange exams. Prior to that, membership of The Stock Exchange was by nepotism and patronage although they still retained the quaint concept of proposer and seconder before being approved for membership.

ICAEW has a very sensible attitude while others are quite proscriptive. The accountancy body expects its members to keep themselves up to date for whatever branch of the profession their incumbents are to follow. The way individuals choose to do that is up to them and they are able, when renewing their membership each year, to self-certify. Other bodies insist on supervision – that is, effectively reporting to a third party, who has been established and approved to check that the individual is indeed keeping up to date.

Professionals should be trusted to ensure that they themselves are able to deliver the advice and/or services that their clients expect. Clients ought to be able to recognise whether or not their coaches or consultants have indeed kept themselves up to date. One view could be that CPD/CPE is used to ensure that the profession in question remains a 'closed shop'. That's an unlikely scenario for coaches, as coaching is a profession with very low barriers to entry.

Readers should forgive an element of cynicism creeping in here! I am merely trying to set a background for a much more important and relevant subject, setting the scene for continuous learning in business. It is not a good thing to set up in business and believe that one can then operate the same way forever. Of course, these days we are spoon fed as consumers. We have plug and play technology. We no longer have to learn how to tune a new radio or television as it's all done for us when we switch on. Even my five-year-old grandson can do it.

Is this a benefit? Of course, as it enables us to spend the time doing more valuable things. Things don't always work out as we expect, though. In 1985 with the coming of Windows 1.0 we were all wondering what we would do with the four days we wouldn't need to work because technology would soon allow us to complete so much in a three-day week. We were setting out to develop activities for our leisure time! Little did we know that the World Wide Web, email and social media would take over our lives both for good and for bad. Do we acknowledge, though, that we don't need to learn about so many things when a couple of clicks will bring us the facts from the cloud and enable us to get on with life without struggling to learn or at least remember those facts?

A lovely vignette about World Wide Web: WWW in Hebrew is ו ו ו Vav Vav Vav, ו Vav is the sixth letter of the Hebrew alphabet, so ו ו ו is 666, the number of the beast. Need one say more? Another saying remembered from a long time ago is, "he who sups with the devil should use a long spoon". It didn't say don't sup with the devil! We have choices, we must make them. There was an advertising campaign recently that tried to show the two sides of the internet, both good and evil. Like everything from fire ('a good servant but a bad master') and shopping (personal viewpoint) there is good and bad in everything. In any case if there wasn't any bad how would we know what 'good' is?

Keeping on top of one's game

Let's get back to the point. However we keep up to date, be it newspapers, the Web, books, lectures, learned papers or, preferably, a mixture of all, we must keep on top of our game. How else are we going to run our businesses, advise others, ensure that we stay ahead of the competition and avoid just being a 'me too'? When we set up businesses we need to allow for the fact that we are starting up and have limited resources. With limited resources, we will, of necessity, have to ensure that we can cover all needs with just a few people. Those few people, including the leader or owner/manager, will need to be able to deliver and to show others how to deliver. That delivery and the business needs will be dynamic and will keep changing. It cannot stand still otherwise it will stagnate. Change and the need for change are vital in any business. In order to change in the right direction, to change for the better, the team will of necessity be obliged to keep up to date, even if it is, of itself, a game changer, such as Apple under the leadership of Steve Jobs.

So, are we, is our business, one that needs to be at the cutting edge or can we motor on as an 'also ran' doing stuff that many others are doing and not making very much by way of profit? Even if we have what could be called an 'ordinary' business, say a cafe or restaurant, we will need to keep up to date with hygiene laws, with the places we obtain our supplies; and unless we are a mere 'greasy spoon' we will even need to be a bit different to keep abreast of the competition along the street and around the corner.

There are extremes in this chapter, from the professional standards to the basic rules of competition, in order to establish that continuous learning is vital at whatever stage or in whatever business we are focused.

We said in an earlier chapter that customers don't know what they want until they get it. No different from the camera phone to Henry Ford's suggestion that if asked, the public would want faster horses. We don't know what we don't know as we've said before. So, how on earth do we push ourselves ahead of the crowd? How do we come up with the snail porridge of the business world? Only by continually learning and by using that learning to be creative and different. But as indicated earlier and as I'll show in a later chapter, we need to allow the learning ingested by the left brain to be shared with the right brain and used in order to be innovative, for interest and for profit. We have to be both innovative and disruptive to streak ahead of the competition and if we don't streak ahead of the competition we will fall behind and be overtaken by them and our competitors.

This is not an easy concept to espouse. We have so much to do in building businesses on a day-to-day basis that the idea of research for research's sake could be considered counter-productive. We're back to the argument about time again. Without continuous learning we will get stuck in a rut, or as one of my US colleagues put it, "a rut is a groove, which is a grave, open at both ends." Clearly, a fate worse than death.

Continuous learning is, of itself, a joy, if you have the mindset that you are subjecting yourself to something new all the time. Thus newness helps elevate your mind, your thinking, even your soul to a higher plane. While Abraham Maslow toned down some of what was in his *Hierarchy of Needs* in later years, it is still absolutely relevant to business people, who are for the most part human beings, who try to elevate themselves if not to the highest levels of self-actualisation, then at least to the level of contribution and significance; they seek recognition by others of their own self-worth. These are the greatest motivators. Employers don't always realise that recognition of an employee is one of the most powerful tools in the motivation armoury. Employees have a need to feel valued in order to help themselves move forward in their careers within or without that particular business. Without motivation, employees move backwards and if they move backwards, so will the business. In fact, in Maslow's terms, 'self- actualisation' merely means, "morality, creativity, spontaneity, problem solving, lack of prejudice, acceptance of facts". I'm not sure, therefore, why some commentators feel that too high an aspiration. (See also page 111).

The path to take

How do we decide on which path of continuous learning to take? If we recognise that we don't know everything, it's quite easy. Just keeping one's eyes open for opportunities to learn and following those opportunities is so valuable and very cost effective. There are a huge number of individuals selling their own brand of knowledge, areas where they have made a particular study that they are willing to share and do so often with free marketing events where huge amounts of learning can be absorbed. It is often not necessary to go on to purchase the programme in order to enhance one's own learning. Although, of course, directing one's focus to a plan of learning for oneself is usually hugely valuable. These people use the drug pusher's technique; they offer you something free to get you hooked. Although I'm not pushing drugs I do feel that the free enticement is something business people should do more to obtain an added advantage.

Incidentally, you will realise that this model is one extensively used in social media. Offer something free to obtain an email address; then offer something cheap to get your audience hooked; then offer something on a subscription basis, which can hook them in for the longer term. Clearly, a subscription basis for a service provides the seller with a really satisfying stream of earnings for the longer term.

Now we see another side to continuous learning. It provides not only a way of keeping up to date but also a new business opportunity. This was far more difficult with the sale of weekly or monthly publications that had to be despatched by post rather than a subscription offer dealt with entirely on line. I wonder how many who are reading this have subscribed to a series of 'learnings' but not even opened the email after a few weeks and allowed those messages to pile up in the inbox or a sub-folder of the inbox 'to be read later'. At least when the weekly or monthly publication dropped through the letter box and lay on the side table it was a loud and visible reminder that there was something to be read.

Social media helps

The vendor as well as the learner can benefit hugely from this opportunity. By hooking people with social media marketing we can reach into their homes and businesses far more effectively. We should be exploiting this concept for ourselves and others; we need to ensure that whatever it is we are selling or buying we continue to keep ourselves up to date. Continuous learning is the lifeblood of business and, as we have seen, need not cost a fortune in time or money. As we all put aside time to be entertained, we can put aside time for 'entertaining learning', as much of it is. In order to ensure marketability, the 'vendors' of learning need to be entertainers too; the word 'edutainment' has even been coined for this concept.

The whole idea is that we open ourselves up to new ideas, we ensure that we are not treading the same old pathways and that we take our businesses forward with new ideas, new concepts, and new products. While much of this is done on a self-help basis, there will be a step-change of the input if the accountant, the poet and the coach from external sources are also utilised and exploited. The accountant will be there to provide information, the poet to provide explanations and the coach to ask the necessary questions. Thus by using all three attributes, both metaphorically and substantively, the business will be helped to grow and to grow much faster than without these additional forces.

While we think of continuous learning as generally bordering on the academic, also remember just how much added value you as a business leader can garner from film, theatre, TV, radio, museums, galleries and sport, from both a spectator's and a participant's point of view.

We can learn merely as a business leader *per se* but also as board member, as someone, who themselves gives talks, writes articles, and – simplest of all – writes blogs. The latter can be done in a few minutes each week and if posted in the right places should evoke responses and learning for oneself. I was asked to give a talk at a business exhibition not long ago. I went on to one of the groups to which I belong on LinkedIn, set the scene and asked for ideas. Within a couple of days, I had received enough material to make three such speeches! That's a great thing about social media – used in the right way, it can produce invaluable content. Sure, one needs to check facts but as a basis for all types of intervention it is invaluable.

The key is seeing beyond today while living in the present. It is essential, as we've said before, to be sensitive not only to what is going on in the here and now but also to what might be, to those concepts that will clearly be manifest in years to come. Of course timing is vital and being too premature can be risky but I wonder whether it is as risky as falling behind with innovation. So, by continuous learning, I don't just mean the continuing professional development that I referred to at the start of this chapter but a never-ending process of continuing business development. Standing still is not an option.

As we've discussed, it is not just receiving the learning, it is the ability to pass it on, whether that be to one's employees, one's colleagues, one's customers or even one's suppliers. As customers ourselves we need to educate our suppliers as to our evolving needs and not just be dictated by them. OK, we can go and find new suppliers, just as we can go and find new customers but how much more satisfying to keep both sets moving along with us. It is true, though, that we can and must, learn from each other. However, the act of passing on our developed knowledge is, as we've seen, also a means of educating ourselves. The development of ourselves, our teams – indeed our companies – must be an over-riding driver towards success, and, as we know, success is a joy in itself.

Training

What about executive MBAs? This has become a very popular choice for young executives who want to get on, but apart from the disruption in companies when staff take time out to go to business school, I wonder whether they actually learn anything of value. As they put it in *The Puritan Gift*, management training often takes away the very aspect of entrepreneurialism that is needed not only in SMEs but in larger corporate entities.

My concern, as theirs, is that such training focuses mainly on the left brain and takes very little account of the creativity and freedom of expression found by exercising the whole rather than just a half of the brain. Sure, it can be considered continuous learning, but as you will realise, I've headed this chapter 'continuous learning' and not 'continuous education' for the reasons already covered.

We need to learn continuously, we need to ensure our teams learn continuously. What's the best way to do this? Certainly, we don't really want them to go back to school. We want them to learn from each other and from their peers. Do we just leave them to their own devices? Do we just tell them that they've got to keep learning or do we plan a programme for them to follow? We keep being told that the younger generations – the Y, the Millennial Generation – are not satisfied with long-term careers like the baby-boomers and Generation X before them.

A lovely anecdote about the difference, which is no doubt ageist, between Generations X and Y – they are like dogs and cats. The dog looks up to his master, who feeds him, looks after him, takes him for walks so he thinks his master is God. The cat on the other hand expects to be fed, expects to be looked after and believes that he, the cat is God! Generations Y and younger believe that they are there to be looked after, to be stroked, as it were and do not have the same loyalty to the business. Not really strange but their prime loyalty is to themselves. Business owners need to realise this and act accordingly. But what has this to do with continuous learning? In earlier years, where the team member looked upon his (and it was mostly his) employment as a job to be done, he tended to do as asked without question and expected to be in the company for years.

Things are quite different today; attitudes are quite different. 'The job' is where the younger person is selling their time for money as before, but that transaction is merely one on the road to success and fulfilment, not just the road to retirement. It has been estimated that people today will have had at least six or seven jobs before they reach the age of 35, which has nothing to do with recessionary times and everything to do with career progression and the stepping stones to ever greater things. So, to keep such people motivated and focused on what the boss wants done, this has to be recognised and encouraged with the right sort of continuous learning by the team members.

Life learning and trust

Perhaps we should recognise that business learning needs to be coupled with life learning; after all, knowledge and information can be much more easily obtained with the existence of the web than ever before. Of course, one needs to take care with information gleaned from sources that are not necessarily exhaustively checked unlike the hard copy *Encyclopaedia Britannica* of my younger days, but how do we know that even with all that publication's exhaustive verification that everything was completely true and accurate? Have we then been taught to be a bit more cynical these days or are we, watched as we are continuously by cameras 'for our own safety and security', rather more cautious than in earlier years? I for one, have a personal credo, that if I trust no one, no one is likely to trust me. So, again, we come back to one of the main causes of disruption in business – lack of trust. So, is that lack of trust we talked about in a previous chapter an effect rather than a cause? It's probably both cause and effect. As Penny Power, in her book *Know Me, Like Me, Follow Me*, expounds, we need to build the relationship in stages so that whether it be in social media on which Penny is primarily focused, or in business generally, we won't get anywhere unless we create that trusting relationship. That applies just as much internally as externally.

Coaching and being coached

If, as we have said, people are going to be continuously moving on, we have to make it part of their role to help others to learn. We have to build into the culture of the company the ethos of continuous learning not just for themselves but also for their peers and their subordinates. The daily task of doing business must, of itself, be a continuous learning process. This is clearly an area where the internal and/or external coach comes in. Again we are talking about the coaching process rather than a mentoring process but we need both in this context. By asking questions we can really find out if they have learned, rather than telling people 'stuff' and either assuming or guessing that it's gone in.

The essence of this message is that bringing in trainers rather than coach/facilitators can be counter-productive, "Oh why do we need this? Can't we just get on with doing the business?" – be it making, selling, developing. Attending sessions for a full or even a half day, whether in or out of the office, can be very frustrating. On the other hand a 60- or 90-minute coaching session either solo or in a group can bestow huge value on the team members. They will go back to their desks feeling empowered and invigorated.

So, what subjects should such coaching cover? Exactly those that we have been talking about so far. We want our teams to be learning on the job about what helps them to do their jobs better, what helps them to grow as individuals, what helps them to extend their capabilities and thus their ability to contribute rather more to the business and to enhance their own chances of success. However, I can hear a little voice whispering in my ear: if they don't know what they don't know, how can they decide what to learn? Great question and one that really underlines the value of coaching rather than training. A good coach will by assiduous questioning find out exactly what needs to be learned, what needs to be discussed, what avenues need to be opened up.

One of my previous coaches Carrie McHale and I used to have a fortnightly telephone session. She has the skill that within about five seconds she would hit on the very topic that I needed to work on. A good coach should equally be able to hit the spot and provide the basis for a really valuable coaching session. Equally, even the employee who doesn't know what he doesn't know will soon be able to assess whether the coach presented to him will have the ability to help. Another of my personal coaches, Hetty Einzig, as well as challenging me here, there and everywhere, really encouraged me to work on the poetry side of the equation.

The power of challenge through 'not understanding'

At this point I would like to come back to an aspect of coaching about which I feel very strongly. I referred in an earlier chapter to the swimmer Mark Spitz whose coach couldn't swim. I feel it is wrong, if not dangerous, for management to choose coaches who 'understand the business'. The whole purpose of a coach is to pull out the client's needs and those needs are not satisfying their learning about that particular business. That is a separate issue and what should be covered by training. By not knowing too much about a particular business or industry sector, the coach, just like the independent non-executive, is able to ask questions which are not obvious, which may appear naive but will encourage the person being coached to open up in such a way as they wouldn't be able to if they were discoursing with a person knowledgeable in their particular business segment.

Another aspect of this is the fallacy of allowing the coachee to choose their coach from a selection presented to them. Far better for the line manager or HR partner to choose someone they think will be appropriate and see if they 'get on'. That way, there is an arm's-length choice, which is usually more powerful than allowing the coachee to select from a group of possibilities. I have seen on many occasions an initial 'dislike' or uncertainty lead to really challenging interventions. A parallel to this is in recruitment where there is a danger that we recruit, or endeavour to recruit, people we like at first interview.

Challenge is one of the most powerful tools in the coach's armoury. It enables the coach to dig ever deeper and to get the person being coached to really look inside themselves to find answers that they really had no clue that they would be able to be clear about in the future; nor indeed that this was something of which they were even aware.

The coach thus opens the coachee to their own innate knowledge, enables them to recognise strengths that they didn't know they possessed and thus in the process become more aware and more able to perform their role in the workplace and also in domestic situations.

Helping the person being coached to be aware of their strengths brings huge added value to the coaching intervention because clearly that individual is then able, with confidence, to tackle increasingly difficult tasks. What a bonus for the company and for the employees themselves. A great book that I refer to for this concept is by Marcus Buckingham: *Now, Discover Your Strengths*. As employers, line managers and bosses, we should encourage the development of strengths as opposed to trying to fill the cracks caused by weaknesses. Far better to focus on the former rather than the latter as it takes less energy and produces far better results.

In my formative years there was an expression, 'learning from Nellie'. As I had an aunt Nellie, my father's youngest sister, I got rather confused by this but found out that I was to sit alongside a senior who knew his stuff and watch and listen. As an accountancy trainee, this is how one learned and later, how one taught. Sure one learned some bad habits too but one was usually put right by one of the partners who would knock out most of these that you'd picked up. You certainly didn't want to follow Mr Livesey, one such partner, who every single day of the five years I was there would call in one of the junior trainees to get him his lunch, 'a ham barm with mustard and a custard', in his pure joyful fulsome Lancashire accent. It never varied. At least it taught one consistency!

Later, in the stockbroking firm, we worked in an open plan office – very *avant garde* for those days – with open microphones, so that we could hear our dealers receiving and placing orders. This helped us understand what was going on, how things were done around there and was part of the learning process. I do get upset walking around offices today. Yes, they are for the most part open plan but so many of the teams are simply not talking to each other. They're either sending emails to the chap across the desk or sitting there with headphones to cut out the noise 'so that they can get on with it' and simply not communicating, not learning and certainly not developing. Sitting with or near one's bosses and one's peers was a key part of one's learning.

Mind you, it had some downsides. These were in the smoking days and if one's boss or one's colleague was a heavy smoker it was totally impossible to give up even if one wanted to. Every time they lit up one was tempted to follow suit. It got even worse when the boss moved on to cigarillos with their pervasive smell. I wasn't able to give up until I became CEO, had my own office and we were hit by Black Monday, 19 October 1987, which I thought was a good opportunity to cut my 60-a-day habit! That was the day the index fell like a stone and after a very buoyant bull market we lost 70% of our business overnight. That was indeed a learning experience but thankfully not a continuous learning experience, just very sobering.

By that time the huge changes in Stock Market regulation had been in place for about 12 months; I had been MD then CEO for about two years. It was a time when, with new rules and the abandonment of self-regulation, my word was no longer allowed to be my bond[8]. The era of compliance had arrived in our fairly cosy and enjoyable environment. It was also the time that American firms had started to come to the UK and make acquisitions of very old established firms. Many names that had been around for two hundred years were swallowed up and it was the end of liquid lunches as we knew them. It was the start of lunch at the desk and earlier mornings than we had been used to. You keep learning new ways of doing business!

One good aspect was that we no longer had personal unlimited liability. That had ended in 1984 when we were also allowed to advertise for the first time. We really didn't know how to handle this. All business up to that point had accrued by personal connections. It was who you knew, not only what you knew, but 1984 brought a new phenomenon; privatisations. One learned to be a media star. The BBC approached us as northern stockbrokers to attend the first of these events, the privatisation of British Telecom (now BT). We held a Q&A

---

[8] *'My Word is my Bond' was the original motto of The Stock Exchange, London.*

session on TV with management, who had been advised not to say anything in case they fell foul of rules prohibiting the extolling of one's company's virtues and values. So, these guys just sat there mute while we, unused to public exposure, had our first experience of being interviewed on live TV. That was indeed a learning experience for which I personally am truly grateful. On the way to the actual event I drove there with a cameraman and an interviewer filming and asking questions, trying hard not to turn around, but among other things being asked if my young daughters were going to be applying for shares. They were 9 and 13 at the time.

Life's events are learning opportunities. Business events are learning opportunities. We need to combine these and interweave with more formal learning be it training, coaching, studying, whatever seems appropriate to the needs of the company, and the needs of the individuals within that company. That learning should go from top to bottom not just be confined to middle management. A grave concern is that the annual budget, while prepared with some allowance for training but often with nothing for top management (for 'the boss'), is probably the line that is deleted first when the board says, 'we've got to cut back'. To my mind this is wholly short-sighted and hardly consistent with the concept of continuous learning.

Visibility as a leader

One of the key stumbling blocks for chief executives is the 'Imposter Syndrome'. It is indeed the case that bosses are expected to know everything and that teams spend time wondering what on earth they do all day. Hence the vital importance of MBWA – management by wandering about. It is absolutely necessary for the boss to relate and personally communicate with the teams on a frequent basis. People need human interaction, which, in my view, doesn't include email but can include handwritten notes, particularly 'thank you's and 'well done's which are highly appreciated if not treasured by staff; one of the best motivators. The concept of handwritten notes has been challenged by those nearer the Millennials but I still believe it's valid because it's different. Keeping people motivated is the best way of keeping them engaged and on board.

Do take care with email; too many people think they can just dash off messages without paying too much attention to spelling or grammar. Just consider these two sentences:

Woman, without her man, is nothing.
Woman, without her, man is nothing.

Just moving one comma can reverse the meaning of the sentence. Be warned.

These are merely my thoughts; since Aristotle, Lao Tse *et al* there have been people speaking and writing about these subjects; sometimes they conflict but that's what debate is about. Lao Tse suggested that the best leaders are those who are invisible. Jim Collins' research showed that those companies with CEOs who were not seeking publicity or the limelight did best. What I feel we are talking about is the difference between the work that has to be done inside the company and that done outside and, in the latter case where the CEO is looking to publicise the company rather than themselves, that is the key.

Vision

Envision -
Help the mind
Entrap the success
That you feel in your
Bones
In your elemental
And deepest
Triumphant victory
For all that you wish for
That you
Yearn for
That you strive with all your
Might

For self
For family
For friends
For employees
For shareholders
For the taxman
Even...
For every stakeholder
In a paradise
On earth
Breaking through the ordinary
And the mundane.

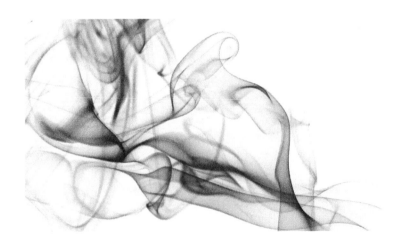

CHAPTER SIX

Focus on vision

Sticking to the picture you have painted
as the ideal future for your business.

I MAKE no excuse for the mention of vision so many times.
It is one of the most important concepts in connection with
running a business that I can think of.

Someone said that vision without action is daydream and
action without vision is nightmare, so it's no good on its own;
but as quoted in *Alice*, unless you have a vision, whether it's
for your business or just for yourself and/or your family, you're
never going to get anywhere. Of course, if you don't want to
get anywhere, enough said!

We need that vision so that whatever we do we can check that
we're on the right track, that we know what we are supposed to

be doing. Not only does the leader need to know where they are headed, it is essential that the team are also fully in the picture, and then they too can be sure that what they're doing is right for the needs of the business. It's the 'why' we're in business, and the 'why', according to Simon Sinek (*Start With Why*), is *the* most important part of doing business, more important than the 'what' (we're doing), more important than the 'how' we're doing it. This is umbilically linked to the 'mission' or, as I prefer to call it, (from Kraig Kramers) the 'customer purpose'. So, the vision is why we're in business for ourselves, and the mission is why we're in business for our customers. Without our customers we have no business so we can see just how important it is that the two are designed to be linked together and are really in alignment.

As enumerated and illustrated earlier, every business needs a business plan, which should start with a clear vision as to what sort of business you and the team are going to build. It should have a timescale; in other words, by when will that business be built? It may be only the first stage of building the 'empire' but it must be achievable within that time looked at from this beginning. We know things can change and it's perfectly reasonable for the vision to change or be changed as time goes on. Indeed it is necessary to take a pragmatic view and allow for change to happen; after all, in business, it would be wonderful if we could foresee the future but owing to the vagaries of climate, of politicians, of the tax regime, of disruptive technology, of fashion, of social mores, of the previously mentioned Black Swans, we cannot. We do not have a crystal ball and even if we did, it would not see everything! So, we need to focus on what we believe is possible for us to achieve in the foreseeable future. In view of all this, as we will see in the next chapter, it is necessary to really focus on the goals and targets that go to make up that Vision and in so doing we achieve our end desires.

Visions tend to be formulated on three-to-five-year time scales. Tom Hill of the Eagle Summit (www.tomhillwebsite. com), an annual symposium, recommends, three-to-six-year scales. Six years splits into 2x3; it also splits not only into 6x1 but also 4x18 months and 18 months is a much better timescale than 12 months; it is far more flexible than 12 months, which tends to be the focus because of accounting synchronicity with fiscal and financial years. How much better if we just look a little further out than the end of the financial year by using an 18-month time scale; time to fix more realistic budgets, time to plan for seasonal patterns, where we can look at repeating a sales strategy and planning on a much more sensible basis. Because of the design, manufacture and distribution of garments, the fashion industry is an example of one forced to have extended timescales.

The parallel is the fixation with quarterly results from listed companies. Yes, investors are keen to know how companies are doing on a fairly frequent basis but how on earth can a three-month period be realistic to assess longer-term plans? Share prices are flexed by P/E ratios (price divided by earnings) and multiplied by a longer-term view, depending on the industry and the view of its quality and sustainability of those earnings. So, engineering might be rated at 10 or 11 times, banks at 8 or 9 and technology companies on 19 or 20, a reflection of how much further out an investor is prepared to pay. In the Far East ratios tend to be even higher, for the reason that the Japanese and the Chinese are happy to focus on rather longer time scales. How much better then, if our smaller companies are able to focus and plan on a considerably more flexible basis, are able to look forward and assess trends without having to change the strategy too frequently, allowing stability in those plans.

Considering the vision

When we start considering our vision, we probably have some preconceptions. We dream of starting a business because of some earlier patterning in our formative years; we see an opening in the market from a perspective of a corporate position that we feel leaves something to be desired. We are someone whose 'element' is a field far from where we are now. We get excited by the prospect of becoming rich beyond the dreams of avarice and we believe that we have the solution. Many times such dreams are, as we all know, just that, but something drives us, something tells us that we can do it and as quoted earlier, if you believe you can, you are right. So we just get on with it!

We get in the zone and can see, feel and breathe the end result. Of course, that's just the start. We 'see' the end result, that is, the vision and we must share that vision, not just to check that it's achievable but to ensure that we have the right people around us, or as Jim Collins puts it, "to get the right people on the bus". I am not suggesting that we need to be messianic about our vision but we do need to express it in such a way that our team really understands what we're talking about, really 'get the message' and really, really, want to be involved. That way we'll get the results we want.

The vision not only encapsulates the dream, it is a focus of the realities of what we want to achieve, the numbers, the results, the questions we need to ask and keep on asking in order for that vision to be brought to fruition. Without all that we will get nowhere. On the other hand (and yes, we've all heard the one about the one-handed accountant) how many really trite and/or woolly visions have we heard and seen about 'being the best in the world widget manufacturer' or similar. What does that mean? Weasel words are not helpful. We must learn to be rather more precise when articulating what our focus is going to be. Size, shape, colour will all come into it.

Profit and cash

We need to know just what will make the business profitable, just what will drive it forward in a cash positive way and, as we've already said, profit is nothing without cash. So, in my view, cash has to be at the centre of what we're trying to achieve. Cash has to be a real focus of our goals and targets. This is, of course, tied to our strategic planning and will be the result of how we set out to develop the business, how we formulate our customer offer, how we ensure that our debtors help us to drive our business forward and, indeed, how we arrange our transactions with our creditors, our suppliers. You will recall my late father's lesson about buying on credit and selling for cash! Cash was another element that we rarely had to worry about as agency stockbrokers as we were just that, agents for our clients. If they didn't pay on the nail, there was no deal.

Although we nearly came unstuck on Black Monday when one of our team allowed a client to really overstretch himself. The initial market correction was felt to be a temporary blip. Indeed it was, but not on such a short timescale as could be covered without immediate action. Our bankers, NatWest (the firm had banked with its forerunner District Bank since the firm's foundation in 1866), were very understanding and helpful. A bit different these days.

On another occasion, we put in applications for a new issue on behalf of a client on the assumption, based on past events, that he would be honourable; but due to a miscommunication he was not honourable and we ended up in court, where the judge described his evidence as 'absurd' and gave judgement in our favour. It did, however, mean we were out of the money for about two and a half years! As they say, 'never assume anything' in business. The client, however, had the last laugh when he was ennobled for something or other many years later!

Do we understand what drives the business? Do we understand how we are to be profitable? Do we understand what creates cash? If not we will never achieve our goals. So, once again, numbers, words, questions combine to get the results we want, the results we need.

Being different

Uniqueness comes into vision; mention was made earlier of competitive advantage, of the unique or emotional selling proposition. This is vital unless you want to be a 'me too' business. Try to be different. Try to ensure that people are drawn to your establishment, your store, your product, because you stand out; perhaps for service, perhaps for the product itself or perhaps because you go out of your way to encourage your customers to remember you in a way that makes them want to buy from you, want to be your customer, to enjoy the experience. Otherwise, they'll just go somewhere else. Sure we can't please everyone all of the time but we can try to please more people than do our competitors.

We've talked about dreams not nightmares but we should also be thinking beyond the ordinary, beyond what was considered possible in the past. We may not have the audacity to be disruptive, to be so different as to sweep away the old boundaries and invent the new, but on the other hand we must endeavour to be different. We must conceive a plan that will achieve all we've discussed otherwise we'll get nowhere. So, what advice do we have to give? I'm a coach, I don't give advice, I just ask the questions; I can't tell you what kind of business to have, what your product will be, your service, how you'll treat your customers, but I can ask you to consider all this and more and to ensure that your plans, starting with vision, are robust.

As we've said, of course you'll make mistakes, as long as, as they say, you always make new mistakes. Doing the same thing over and over and expecting a different result, the first sign of madness, et cetera, et cetera. That's why it's not wrong for you to modify your vision from time to time as you experience market or other changes. However, you always need to be the strong questioner before making such changes. Have things fundamentally changed or is it just a bit more difficult than you thought? Have you built your business too quickly on the back of one major customer perhaps because you had that customer in mind when you first decided to enter that marketplace? However, have you found that this particular customer is unique and you are effectively a division of that business?

If so, you might need to think again or make sure that you are putting yourself in an indispensable position, by building relationships not only with VITO, the very important top officer, (see *Selling to VITO* by Anthony Parinello), the decision maker, but also their colleagues at as many different levels as you can establish.

Business plan

The vision is the first section of the business plan shown in Chapter 2. The next section is the mission, as mentioned earlier in this chapter, then follows, competitive advantage, as discussed in Jaynie L Smith's book, *Creating Competitive Advantage*. What makes you different? What makes your business so different as to really magnetise your customers? Are you the only one that does what you do? According to Jaynie, the more 'onlys' the better. However, as I've said, it's not only the 'onlys' that differentiate, it's the 'why?' It's that emotional pull; it's the thing that makes people queue overnight outside Apple stores, just to be the first to get yet another phone. And, yes, I'm typing this on an iPad but it's not the latest model, although I have just uploaded and installed the latest operating system!

Strategy to reach your vision

Ok, you've decided what it is that you're going to build and what you're going to provide your customers and why they're going to come to you and to no one else. But what is your strategy? And how are you going to work it out? Are you going on an 'away day' to do the brain storm with your accountant, your poet and your coach? Are you going to sit in the forest to be lost in thought? Are you going to attend one of my Unlocking Creativity™ workshops to help you work out how you will get from where you are now to where you want to be? Are you going to attend lectures and seminars or have you already done so? Have you consulted with your mastermind group, real or virtual?

Have you read Collins, Covey, Handy, Peters, Maister, *et al* or, have you just worked it all out 'on a beermat'? – with apologies to my friend Mike Southon. Whatever strategy you choose to help you design your strategy, you're going to need one or, once again, you'll get nowhere. Doing all this stuff in isolation or even doing an executive MBA but having no time to create your strategy let alone get on track and achieve your goals, means it will be wasted. You can see how important it is to have a great vision, a sensible and evocative mission and – with a fair wind and some realistic thinking time – you and your team will work out the strategy you will need to follow to achieve the success you seek.

We have talked about 'the element', being in the zone. Does your vision reflect those concepts? In other words, will you be able to 'float' through, be 'above' the everyday, 'on the business' not 'in the business'? If not, there may be a problem waiting to pounce and hit you where it hurts. It is absolutely vital that, whatever business you are aiming to build, you set yourself up with the right conditions, with the right aspects, otherwise anything that can go wrong will go wrong (known as Murphy's Law). With that concept, the idea of a Black Swan swimming into view at any time, disruptive marketing from competitors and any number of blockages to your success, you must be able to rise above it all.

You must set up a business structure that will enable you to take all this in your stride, to have a team to which you can delegate, otherwise all you will be doing will be managing, or worse, administering, not leading your business. We are really going to have to watch out if companies like Amazon are developing drones to deliver packages weighing 2 kg at 50 mph. Not sure how they envisage doing this to high-rise blocks of flats but who knows what's coming your way very soon.

We said before that everything must have a process, whether it is for garnering and husbanding cash, driving sales, leading the team by managing the space you use; so inevitably, before starting to actually do any business it is essential that you *plan* ahead and work out just what this business you are about to build is going to look like at every stage. The detail need not be laid out in such a way as to exhaust your imagination, but the subset to your vision should be clear in your mind and again shared with your team. Once more, let's not be anal about this, use your creative imagination. Be aware of your team's strengths and ensure that you set things up so that they can be used to maximum effect.

Of course, as time goes on you will see the errors but if your structure is right you will be able to adjust for those errors along the way. How do you make sure that everyone buys into your vision? How do you ensure that the team is working towards what you have decided is to be achieved? By having them alongside of you all the way; by having got on board the right people with the right skills and with the right attitudes. Once you have done this you will be far better placed to delegate.

Your vision should be tested almost to destruction. Every aspect should be reviewed by the team and adjusted where necessary. This way you will have the template, the roadmap for success. You have your roadmap, you have your strategy for following that map, you have the team to help you follow the map and you have the premises to operate from – this applies just as much to start-ups in garages, back bedrooms or leased or borrowed space. You have a cash pot scraped together from your savings, from friends, from family, probably not from banks but possibly from crowdfunding. You won't have achieved this if you haven't been able to share an exciting, plausible and realistic vision.

Milestones

Having bought into your vision alongside your team, having recognised your timescale, there will be expectations of milestones towards your success. Set out from the beginning your communication strategy, how often you're going to keep them in touch with progress and then stick to that schedule.

If they know that you will keep them in the picture and when, you won't be at risk of having to stop the business flow to answer questions, to be interrupted during the time you need to be focusing on driving the business. Be sure to set expectations that things will inevitably go wrong and that you might be looking for more cash before success is established. Try to let there be no surprises and make this a golden rule in the company. There's not much worse for a boss than to be surprised. You need to be on top of your game and thus really establish 'no surprises' as a continual mantra in the business.

Of course, there will be surprises. You will be surprised by something new in the marketplace, by the reaction to your latest offering from your best customer, by something your best employee throws at you. After all, it's usually your best employee that will be poached, unless you continually share your vision and that person and their colleagues recognise what you are doing, why you are doing it and how you are doing it. They want to feel an important part of 'what' and 'why', otherwise, however well paid, they will become demotivated and move on, so make them feel that they are an integral part of the vision, which indeed they are, if the set-up is correct.

However, even if you believe your vision to be correct, your team likewise believe in it, and your investors have taken it on board, you do need to check carefully before setting out on the road that your assumptions about market size, about the landscape, about the strengths of your team, about your own and the team's credibility, are indeed correct. Once again, if it can go wrong, it will. So maximum communication at all levels and from all sides to ensure that everyone, including you, is up to speed. It's a very tall order.

Don't let all this put you off. Remember, if you believe you can, you're right! So move, get on with it and be a success. You've designed your strategy, you've set your targets and you've designed your plans to achieve those targets. You need to have a laser-beam focus on those targets so that they will be achieved. You can see from all this, though, just how important it is to have that clear vision, to see the way forward, to have all your team and stakeholders see the way forward and with their help and support you will get there in the expected time.

How your customers see your purpose

We spent a few moments earlier in this chapter referring to the concept of customer purpose or mission but we didn't dwell on the way we came to the decision as to what that mission would be. This is why some commentators prefer to focus first on mission and then on vision. They aver that until you know what it is you are going to do for your customers, how can you know what sort of business you're going to build? The answer to that is the concept of 'why'. It's far more important to know why you want to do something than just what you are going to do. So, having decided 'why' by designing the vision, we can now concentrate on what we are going to do for the marketplace, for the customers.

Do we know the size of the market? Do we know the size of the competition? Again, how will we differentiate ourselves?

As far as our target customers are concerned, why on earth should they come to us? Have we the best product? Do we offer the best service? Do they just like the way we relate to them? Often, much of that just cannot be incorporated in a procurement process where price is apparently the only criterion. So, therefore, we have to, in some way, show them that price should not be an issue. It's no good focusing solely on price if delivery times are dysfunctional, quality is often substandard, packaging is a weak point and so on. Try hard to show that what you do for your customer is why they should be doing business with you and no one else.

You will no doubt be aware of the road haulier, Eddie Stobart, who decided to go right against the trend by ensuring that his trucks were always spotlessly clean and his drivers always smartly uniformed. It not only brought huge publicity it also brought a following from those who wanted their goods delivered in a 'smarter' way. At the time, no one else had even considered that this was a relevant and valid way of going about the daily task. In time many others followed his lead and it became a 'me too', but for a while it was a business winner. So, you must always continue to be ahead of the game and every time you think of something new, you should be planning the next move, just like a game of chess. There will always be someone out there aiming to beat you at your own game. It's thus no good resting on your laurels. You need at least one person in the team who will come up with ideas for you. If your team is small and you can't afford the specialist help in house, consider all the ancillary businesses that can help you improve yours by providing such services by the day or by the hour. They need not be excessively expensive. Again look at the return on your investment. I'm thinking of businesses like the FD Centre (part-time finance directors), Your Right Hand Finance Team (suppliers of bookkeeping and similar services), People Puzzles (for HR and personnel matters) and The Marketing Team. There are any number of IT wizards and let's not forget that keeping up to speed with the latest technology can put you streets ahead of your competitors.

Social media and business development

I guess that takes us back to social media and I'm not going to enumerate the many opportunities there are via the multitude of social media sites to connect with customers, suppliers and even competitors (because they can lead to other customers). Don't just look at LinkedIn, Twitter and Facebook but also at the myriad of other links to the virtual community. Much of this costs nothing except time. The same applies to your outputs via blogs, a great way of reaching the audience you know about as well as the audience you don't know. As I've said, by spending just a few minutes a week your sales message can be exposed to a multitude of individuals and businesses. Also, think sideways; don't always blog about what your business can do. Paul S, a former Vistage member who runs a technology business providing dealing systems and mobile communications, writes about gastronomy and golf.

So, sit down with your team and work out just what you and they can be doing about developing business. Whether or not you have a business development director, a sales director, a marketing director or they have teams, it is my belief that everyone in your company should be and can be a 'salesperson.' Everyone should be given the responsibility of contributing towards the sales effort. After all, no sales, no business. On the other hand, don't promote your best sales person to be sales manager, no matter how much they crave the promotion. The skills are entirely different. By all means give them an enhanced title but make sure they are still responsible for bringing in the sales not managing the rest of the team; sales people are loners. Nurture that concept.

Another word of warning; when trying to work out your budgets, don't overestimate the sales that will be achieved. Your sales people will in any case push back on the targets set and either ask for a reduction or refuse to allow you to raise prices. Sales people hate the idea of raising prices but as the money guys will tell you, the leverage of raised prices is enormous. By raising prices only a fraction, actual sales can be allowed to drop far more than you would expect. Equally, drop your prices and you need to make rather more sales to make up than you would expect. Do the sums.

We've just said that everyone should be involved in business development and sales just as everyone should have taken on board the reality of the company's vision and let me repeat that, it's the company's vision not just yours. That is absolutely essential. So it's one team, one focus, all contributing towards the success you desire, all therefore able to enjoy the rewards of that success.

My son-in-law, a partner in a mid-term accounting firm, still does his business development in what some might see as an old-fashioned way. He plays golf with potential clients. By so doing he has, he says, a captive audience for three or four hours!

Focus on Targets and Goals

Having set a goal
To plan
And write
A book
In 90 days
How on earth
Can this be done?
By the utmost focus
On the chapters
The sections
The pages
And...
Lo... It is
Done.
How little different
To run
To steer
To lead

The business
With focus and
Not
With
Busy-ness
Achieving success
For the product
For the service
For the owners
And for all those
Who yearn
For that
Joyous
And emotional
Success
As a given
With thanks.

CHAPTER SEVEN

Focus on targets and goals

Sticking to what makes up,
and leads to, the future ideal.

WE HAVE spent some considerable time looking at vision. As we've said before, vision without goals is a daydream, while goals without vision are a nightmare. So, we have to spend as much time on both. We have our vision. What does it take in terms of goals and objectives to realise that vision?

How do goals focus the vision? What do we have to do to ensure that they are the right goals for that vision? There are a number of stories, which may or may not be apocryphal, but even if they are I don't think that matters. The story goes that at Harvard Business School, the 4% who formulated their goals in writing and shared them with others (another way to focus), achieved a total wealth that exceeded the total of the remaining 96%. I don't know if this is true or not but it makes a good story and, indeed, it has the ring of truth about it and it's logical. It feels right, too!

For the rest of this chapter, I'm going to assume that it is true. We have seen just how important it is to have a vision. We have suggested that without such a vision, it will not be possible to build a successful business; to have everyone involved in helping to build that business. We have talked about the janitor at Cape Canaveral feeling that he was part of the vision that he was helping to put a man on the moon.

One hears far too many times that the boss feels they can't possibly let the staff know that the aim is to sell the business in due course. I feel this is terribly short-sighted. Their reasoning is that they believe that if the team realise that the business is to be sold that they would be out of a job. What distinctly old-fashioned thinking! We've already recognised that teams these days don't see themselves in the company forever. They too want to believe that helping to build a company will bring rewards to them as well as to the shareholders. Bring them in to the vision with the prospect of some part of the reward when the company is indeed sold. Share the ambitions and that will certainly motivate and introduce a culture that rewards loyalty and ensures retention, one of the biggest issues facing growing businesses. There is no need to make them equity partners, only to set up a perfectly legal deferred bonus scheme which shares in the eventual sale. "If you're around when we sell, there will be a share of the overall rewards." It doesn't need to be the lion's share.

Thus, with that in mind, the goals can be formulated taking that concept into account. The authorities recognise this and have made allowance for tax-efficient methods to achieve this. Thus, a company can formulate its goals to take the ultimate eventuality into account without the proprietors being concerned that their take will be too aggressively diluted. Indeed, the prognosis is that with such a structure the overall rewards will be enhanced and in practice there will be no dilution at all because the whole team is working towards the same vision, the same goals.

So, what should the goals be and how should they be structured? Goals should, without question, be formulated in such a way as to bring alignment of all the factors that will drive business success. Everyone must be aiming for the same result, for the same target. The best way to ensure this is by espousing the concept of the balanced scorecard, referred to earlier. The original format was as follows:

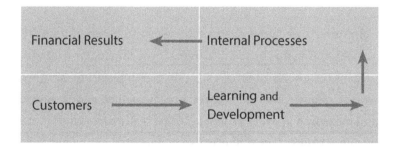

Later they developed a more comprehensive format providing a clearer route to results ever bearing in mind that by the time you have the results it is really too late! For example in sales:

Driver (actions)	⟶	Training/ field visits/recruitment pipeline
Intermediary driver/outcomes	⟶	Sales force performance
Outcomes (results)	⟶	Actual sales

Thus, by setting goals that inspire, that support the whole business and that support each other, there is a much better chance of driving towards better and more acceptable results. In order to achieve key results, with interim key result indicators (KRIs) we are much more likely to perform in this way if we have the right set of KPIs (key performance indicators). By way of example, if we set out to achieve a full-year sales target, a key result, of say, £3m, then we need a quarterly KRI of, subject to seasonality impact, £750,000. A daily or weekly KPI breaking down the monthly sales target will be measured by, for example, the number of sales calls actually made because we know that over a period of time there will be a certain number of sales calls to be made to achieve an overall level of sales.

In order to achieve that, there needs to be an amount of actual training for the team to make those targets, or, for there to be a certain number of calls per meeting set up. In other words a really robust structured process, which can be tested and measured at every juncture. To be really successful, every business needs a suite of processes, ones that are robust, can be measured regularly, can be understood by all involved and understood in such a way that everyone, just like the janitor, can understand what has to be done to achieve the required results.

Key performance indicators (KPIs)

We have talked about the importance of cash. To emphasise, a cash KPI should be incorporated into every process, into every measurement of success. Not what the cost of an action will be but what will be the impact on cash by every action. In many cases the direct impact may be nil but the indirect aspect could be quite large.

To state the obvious, goals or targets focus the mind, goals or targets bring deadlines when such deadlines are incorporated into the goals adding 'by when' the goals need to be achieved. Targets enable people to be held accountable for their actions and for their results. Their colleagues, their management, will know how they're performing. Thus targets form the next piece of the jigsaw of the overall business plan, which leads from vision, customer purpose, competitive advantage, strategy, through to targets and goals; the 'what?', the 'why?', the 'how?' and back to the 'what?'. However, according to Sinek, the most important is the 'why?' Although, ironically, as a coach, one needs to be very sparing in the use of the question 'why?' because it can come over as a bit aggressive or even pejorative.

Goals can be formulated using past experience; a calculation of possible outcomes based on market intelligence and on experience but always with the knowledge of what your team is capable of achieving. It is absolutely useless to use guesswork based on the dream. How often, in assessing businesses in which to invest, have we seen 'dream sheets' rather than robust business plans that follow the best practices of a rigorous planning process? It is certainly easy to set out the steps to formulating a sound plan. It is rather harder to ensure that the plan will be able to live up to its promises.

Critical success factors (CSFs)

One can't say too often that by the time you have the results it's too late to do anything about them. So, we need also to understand and consider CSFs – yes, another TLA, three-letter acronym! This one refers to critical success factors. What do these imply? How do they relate to your business? In the airline industry, one of the real CSFs is turnaround time. How long does the aircraft have to be on the ground before it takes off again? The shorter the time taken, the more efficient the process, the lower the costs and, particularly for short-haul, the more flights can be achieved in a given period.

As I'm writing this, I'm reflecting on a short-haul flight I took only yesterday. My flight was called well before the plane due to take us back home was available and even before it had landed. Passengers queued to present their boarding passes, went through a doorway and then had to stand in line while the arriving passengers disembarked, baggage was offloaded, new baggage loaded. It's clear why passengers are encouraged by extra charges to have carry-on bags only and no stowage bags. Thus, clearly, passengers are encouraged to share the vision of the airline in question by suffering inconvenience themselves! The problem with flying, which whisks you from A to B in a very short time, is the amount of time you are obliged to waste at both A and at B!

So, what are the CSFs for your business? What makes you more successful each time period, more successful than your competitors? What CSFs ensure that your teams are motivated and retained? How do you legislate for external events over which you have no control, the Black Swans, the idea of being 'fooled by randomness' another Nassim Nicholas

Taleb concept? We cannot be prepared for everything. We can, however, be prepared for the fact that things are unlikely to work out exactly as we planned, be they budgets, be they the way human beings behave, whether those human beings are your staff, your customers, your suppliers, your politicians. Thus it is necessary to reassess budgets on a regular basis, to re-forecast your expected outcomes to ensure that you plan better and more often, so that you know as far as is possible your likely cash pot during the next few months.

Quarterly priorities manager

Ally this to a concept known as 'quarterly priorities manager' (q.v. Kraig Kramers, *CEO Tools*). Use this chart for each area and each senior manager in the top team. It is up to them how far down to take it.

Priority Rank	Current Priority for quarter ending: [31 March]	Progress and current status	New priority for quarter ending: [30 June]
1			
2			
3			
4			
5			

Quarterly Priorities Manager

At the beginning of each quarter (a month is generally too short, a year too long), set out in brief detail what your prime focus is for that quarter in a ranked series of actions. At your regular team meeting, everyone reports on where they are up to for the quarter. Set out alongside those actions the further actions you will be pursuing in the following quarter. Thus you will really focus on current goals but at the same time there will be recognition, a cognisance, of what's coming up in the near future. You can thus double-check how things are going. Of course, unless you have a crystal ball or are a particularly tuned-in individual, it is unlikely that you will be able to foresee the unexpected. You can, however, learn to expect the unexpected. The problem is, of course, that entrepreneurs are congenitally structured to be optimistic. If they weren't, they wouldn't start businesses. So, it is likely that they will tend to expect that things will turn out alright!

As humans, we do have several human needs. The original work on this topic was done, as mentioned before, by Abraham Maslow and published in 1943 as *A Theory of Human Motivation*. The theory is usually shown as a pyramid or hierarchy, with safety and security at the bottom rising through love, belonging and esteem with self-actualisation at the top.

Maslow implied that unless an individual rose through these levels they would again become discontented. So, we always strive for something better for ourselves. That is not necessarily in material things; in fact, materiality is unusual. A poet must write poetry, a musician must make music, an artist must paint to ultimately be happy. Tony Robbins has another interpretation; he shows a paradox whereby we crave both certainty and uncertainty, the former to ensure stability, the latter to ensure variety in our lives. We subsequently desire to make a contribution and to grow. Since Maslow, there has been a huge amount of scholarly work done, some showing that he was not necessarily right. Indeed he entered the debate himself. However, I feel that we all need stimulus and a feeling of achievement in order to be and to feel successful. Thus, the targets that are the subject of this chapter not only help our businesses grow, they help us to grow as individuals within and without those businesses.

Hierarchy of Needs

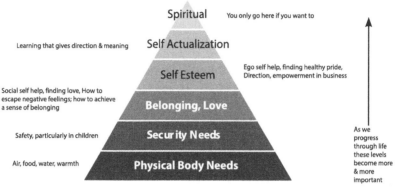

Learning that gives direction & meaning

You only go here if you want to

Ego self help, finding healthy pride, Direction, empowerment in business

Social self help, finding love, How to escape negative feelings; how to achieve a sense of belonging

Safety, particularly in children

Air, food, water, warmth

As we progress through life these levels become more & more important

Abraham H Maslow © 1968

There is certainly a parallel outside the business world in the arts, be they music, drama, dance, painting. The proponents of those arts clearly desire to achieve success in much the same way as we do in business only it's a different platform. We all strive for the ultimate, for the magnificence of self-actualisation be it a sterling performance of Rachmaninov's *Piano Concerto No. 2* or the sale of the company for a few million or the passing on of that business to the next generation.

Goals, targets, I've tended to use these words interchangeably. I've even changed the title of this chapter from 'Focus on Targets' to 'Focus on Goals and Targets'. Is there any difference? Does it matter? Gino Wickman calls them 'rocks'. He takes this term from Steven R. Covey and the concept of putting the rocks in the jar or bucket first otherwise neither the pebbles, nor the sand, nor will the water fit. But, if you put the rocks in first then everything will fit. The conclusion is, do the big and important things first and then you'll find everything else follows; but if you do the small stuff (which someone else said "don't sweat") you'll never get the big and important tasks completed. On the other hand, by using the Wickman terminology, my feeling is that my metaphors are becoming inextricably mixed. So, I prefer goals rather than rocks!

According to the same dictionary we used earlier:

Target, noun:
1. A person, object, or place as the aim of an attack
2. A board marked with a series of circles sharing the same centre aimed at in archery or shooting
3. A goal or result which one aims to achieve: a sales target.

Target, verb:
1. Select someone or something as an object of attention or attack
2. Aim or direct something

Phrases on (or off) target succeeding (or not succeeding) in hitting or achieving the thing aimed at.

So, it's a 'thing', something to aim at rather than something big that needs to be done. I like to believe that in the context of our business plans, these are the objectives that we need to reach in order to succeed, in order to build our businesses. We have goals and targets in our sights, as the dictionary says; we can have, for example, a 'sales target'. Of course, we must have sales targets. It's no good being in business without them. How do we choose the right target to aim for, though? Do we start with what we believe we can achieve in a given period or do we start with what we need to achieve in order to succeed with our plans? Perhaps we should start at both ends but we all know that management will want higher targets than that which the sales force will be prepared to commit to. Human nature creeps in again!

In football and other sports, the goal is a fixture, guarded by an individual supported by the rest of the team, at which a ball or other object is aimed. Elsewhere my goal may be to win a gold medal by hitting the target with my rifle. I use this as an example not because I'm any good at shooting but because one of my clients, Julie O, a veterinary surgeon who founded and runs a training school for veterinary nurses, rifle shoots for England!

It doesn't seem important what we call it as long as everyone knows what our focus of achievement is and how it is to be measured. Currently, my goal is to finish writing this book of between 200 and 250 pages before I go to Spain on a business trip. My target is the finished work and that's also my vision. The whole reflects the concept of SMART; goals need to be Specific, Measurable, Achievable, Relevant, Timely.

There are currently four people I coach who are working on the fulfilment of an MBO (management buyout). Each has reached this stage in their career by a separate and distinct route. Each is managing director of a company where they are the brains but are not the majority shareholder of the company. Each has this as their current goal and beyond, a further goal to continue to build and ultimately sell the business to create financial freedom. We talked earlier about BHAGs. These are big goals but not, in their view, hairy or audacious, just a natural progression from where they are now to where they want to be. At the time of writing they are at different stages, but from my perspective, all are on track. This is their focus. This is their vision.

Business relationships

'Make love' to the sound guy
So I've been told
Just so that he
Will enhance your voice
When on stage
Or
At least, won't let it be
Distorted.
In business 'tis the same
We have to
'Make love'
So that
Our counterparts will

In turn
'Love' to
Help us.
It matters not
Be they
A customer
A shareholder
A member of the team
A supplier or
Indeed,
The taxman...
Who cometh.

CHAPTER EIGHT

Business relationships are the key

Developing and nurturing those who can help you and who, you in turn, can help.

BUSINESS RELATIONSHIPS are one of the most vital keys to success. Without them, you will be working in a vacuum. The relationships I am referring to are both internal and external. Let us start with external relationships. These are clearly vital in order just to do business. We need to work with customers, suppliers, service providers, professional service providers, HMRC, the community, investors, share-holders, bankers, trainers and coaches, peer groups. The list is quite extensive and not exhaustive but there is one thing all these people have in common. The better we get on with them, the more support we're likely to get from them. And, yes, I do include HMRC in that context. By building rapport, by understanding their needs as well as one's own, we can make huge progress in building and sustaining our businesses. This process needs to start on day one.

Some people are better at this than others. If we start with the premise that people go into business to provide the service or the product that truly excites them, then that is their focus and joy. However, it is the outsiders apart from the team that we'll come to later that will all join in to help us achieve what needs to be achieved. We have to find those we can work with, we have to build and nurture the relationship. We also have to reciprocate and help them succeed in their chosen field. If we do so, if we contribute to their success, they will in turn help us to succeed. Of course you can be ruthless in business. It's not my way and, in my view, it may work for a time but it will not be sustainable.

In sales, you have to find VITO, the very important top officer, as we've said earlier. This is the decision maker who may or may not agree to buy what you have to sell. You also have to ensure that your team build relationships with their team so that if anything happens to any one of them there are always substitutes upon whom you can call for that vital decision. It's not only in sales that VITO has to be searched out, found and nurtured, it's also in vital areas like your service providers, your IT support, your accountants, your legal advisers, etc.

Without outside help and outside help from some very important people you'll get nowhere. We're back to the concept of communication tools we talked about earlier. Just because we can communicate with electronic equipment it doesn't mean that we should rely entirely and exclusively on those bits of kit; the iPhone, the Blackberry, the Samsung Galaxy. In fact the less we rely on them the better. Yes, use them but don't rely on them. Learn or relearn to interact face to face, eyeball to eyeball, with your contacts and with your interlocutors.

Having encouraged the use of social media earlier, I'm not suggesting for one moment that you eschew social media and all the amazing IT equipment that is available but don't be like the groups of teenagers you see sharing space together but only communicating via their smartphones. As humans we need, we benefit from and we grow from human interaction. This applies in business as in the social arena and as business is part of life (as Charles Handy said) and as life and business are more and more interconnected and intertwined, the more important it is to maintain the real and not just virtual coexistence. Use the stuff as support, as a major tool, but not as the only means of interaction.

In fact, I have a vision of such electronic communication not being interaction at all at the really meaningful level. After all you can't have a drink or dinner with a piece of electronic equipment, not yet anyway! As Eddie Hillier, a former member of one of my business groups, was fond of saying "you can't get your hair cut on the internet". He said that in 1999; it's still true 16 years later. Of course, it is possible for a surgeon in New York to remotely perform surgery on a patient in Los Angeles using a robot and a camera so I suppose technically it would be possible for a barber to do the same. I think, somehow, that the cost effectiveness would be less than optimum. So we're back to costs and margins and the fact that they too are a consequence of the type of interaction we're discussing and, yes, the cost of a dialogue may direct the type of interaction but money is not the only cost to be considered.

The nurturing process

So, how do we nurture our business relationships? By using what Daniel Goleman called the emotional quotient, or EQ. Some have it more than others. It is an ability to 'get on' with people, to understand them, to make them feel that they want to do business with us, not to be put off by our aggressive or unbending attitude. We give them the impression that we value what they have to offer and in turn they will understand that they can gain by treating us in a like manner. Now, not to be misunderstood: when we're negotiating, we're not going to give the impression that we'll roll over like pussy cats. We can, however, be personable, be relational and in so doing may well put them off guard and grant us a better deal than might have been expected. We may be the seller and of course we will want to be 'nice' to the buyer but we do need to challenge them, they do need to see that what we have to offer will enhance their own business, that they'll be getting the bargain.

In selling, in the last fifty years or so, the received wisdom has moved from selling the benefits, through selling the solution, to the current thinking of challenging the buyer to find a better product or service at a better price. However we do it, the key is the relationship. Once again, it's finding (know me), listening (trust me) and doing business (follow me).

Listening

That leads back to the concept of listening. How often do we really listen to what we are being told? How often are we taken 'out of the room' when someone is talking by something that they said. It reminded us of something we had forgotten to do, something we realised we ought to do, something that happened a long time ago. What we need to do in those circumstances is to make a note (can be mental, but better written) and get back into the room as quickly as possible and really focus attention on what is actually being said.

This does, of course, work both ways in that when speaking we need to be succinct, to allow the listener to absorb and not be side tracked by too much information. They can always ask for more if we present in the right way. This is all part of relationship building. Listen hard, attentively, intuitively and intelligently. Try to get as much out of what is being said by the other person. That is certainly the way to building a better relationship. Please don't just 'hear what they say'. Understand their meaning; relish what you're being told. Sure you'll meet people who are outright bores. Don't do business with them. There's always someone else to deal with. If they really are bores, they'll go out of business anyway and not be able to sustain their supply or sell the goods that you've sold them. Be selective.

In my opening poem for this chapter, I referred to 'love'. That is not romantic love; it is a warmth, a feeling, an openness, a relational connection that creates mutual attitudes on which to build long-term business relationships that are really of mutual benefit. People stay in peer groups for an average of over five years because they have built such relationships they value, ones that they wish to continue from both a receiving and a giving perspective. We often learn as much on occasion by offering advice to another as we learn by receiving it ourselves.

Networking

Listening skills are absolutely vital when it comes to networking, an essential part of building external relationships. Unfortunately, there is a lot of rubbish talked about networking. Fortunately there is some good stuff too. A variant on the mastermind group discussed in Chapter 11 is the breakfast club, such as BNI where small business people go to network and meet likeminded individuals for the cross referral of business. Some are very popular and effective; others less so. The good ones have got past the idea that they are trying to sell to each other. They are building relationships whereby they can introduce the others to those they encounter.

On the social media front, there is LinkedIn. This is a very powerful online network of people who have 'connected' with each other. Very useful for getting introductions to those whom you would like to meet but don't know personally. It is also helpful to follow up on people you've met but who might have disappeared from the company where you originally met them. Some people will link to anyone; my preference is to link with people I've met or to whom I have been introduced. I suppose that's again a reflection of upbringing!

The other powerful type of connection is that of the 'ambassador', the one with whom you have done business in the past and who has a favourable impression of you and your services. This is separate from them putting testimonials on LinkedIn, it is more these people's inclination to mention your name and produce introductions without you setting the pace although you probably do have to ask in the first place.

Internal relationships

So much for external relationships. What about internal ones? These are as important, if not more important in achieving business success. As a boss, as a business leader, you must nurture and develop your team in a very similar way to the way you interact with those outside the business. Later, we will discuss recruitment and, of course, recruiting the right people – 'getting the right people on the bus' is paramount in building a successful business. This chapter will now deal with the relationship you have with your team, with those people who are already on the bus.

The establishing, the building, the motivating, the retention of your team all depend on your relationship with them both as a team and as individuals. You are their boss but you are also responsible for their wellbeing both directly and indirectly, by law, whether you have an in-house HR department or you use the services of an external provider. The buck stops with you, so it is vital that you understand what it takes to have the right and appropriate relationship with them.

Be tough, no-nonsense, demanding, yes, but also visionary and in such a way as the team will have the utmost respect and admiration for you. That doesn't mean you need to do everything; in fact the less you actually do the better. You have to get the right team about you. You have to be great at delegating. Your longer-term aim should be to make yourself redundant. You should be spotting your successor early on.

In my case, I joined the firm at 23 and by 26 I was referred to quietly as 'the Dauphin', the heir apparent, even though I wasn't appointed MD until fifteen years later. I spotted my successor shortly after.

Delegation

One of the biggest complaints I hear from clients is the difficulty they have in delegating; this coupled with the lack of time they have to do anything. They don't seem to be able to see the connection! If only they'd learn to delegate more they'd have much more time to deal with the real stuff, the 'rocks' referred to previously. The key to delegation is relationship with one's team and its individual members. Again it's trust.

If we build a good relationship by trusting people, by helping them to learn to do what you do, and yes, that takes time but a lot less time than you are continually and forever spending, then you will be freeing your time and you will be seeing that what needs to get done is indeed done. If we don't trust them or we don't trust ourselves, we'll stay stuck in a rut of 'no time, no progress'. How often have we heard the cry, "by the time I've shown them what to do, I could have done it myself"? Of course that's true, but you only have to show them once or at the most twice and you no longer have to spend the time doing it yourself. As Aleksandr Orlov, the marketing meerkat, says, 'simples'.

However, it's not just you, the business leader, that needs to form and nurture relationships in the business. You need to make sure that everyone is involved in the process and it should be a process; one that will ensure that from top to bottom and from side to side people get on with each other and thus make more efficient teams and departments. By this I don't mean that they should be 'bosom' pals, always socialising together, although there is usually no harm in that. All that matters is that the relationships have been built so that they understand each other, understand each other's strengths, weaknesses and needs in the business. They don't even have to like each other, just get on!

I have been called upon on numerous occasions to coach senior executives who are one or two down from the main board in larger organisations, where their biggest concern is what they refer to as 'managing upwards'. In other words they want their line managers to understand them better, to realise just what they're capable of, to be able to see that they (the more junior) are capable of continuing to climb the ladder. They want to be able to tell their bosses what we referred to earlier, that every boss should be nurturing themselves for redundancy by growing their people. It's a dialectic that the subordinate often feels what the superior ought to feel and to put into practice. Is it that the senior doesn't recognise this? Or is it the case that they are afraid of their own position, that they might be considered superfluous to requirements by the ultimate arbiter, the CEO? It should be remembered that the CEO is also vulnerable in this regard. In SMEs with a CEO owner, it can of course be more, not less, complex because the boss is the owner and thus will find it much more difficult to 'let go'.

The best leaders allow themselves to be vulnerable and also allow themselves to be seen as not knowing everything. That way they can build a team that punches above its weight because it is not moving at the pace of the boss, it is not inhibited by what it doesn't know it doesn't know. It's more likely that the boss needs the coaching rather than the subordinate!

Thus, the relationship building comes from the top, by example and by strategy. The structure and growth of the organisation is nurtured and developed by the building of great relationships within as well as without. So, how do we go about ensuring that this happens? Again, referring to Patrick Lencioni's work, *The Five Dysfunctions of a Team*, we must ensure that the team is a structure based on mutual trust. The whole team must trust each other, must trust the boss, must trust the rest of the organisation. There must be what Stephen MR Covey calls the 'Speed of Trust' – it's the lubricant that enables things to happen and to happen fast. This goes hand in hand with the ability to delegate, the confidence to delegate. Where does that confidence begin? It begins with oneself. It seems to follow that if you, as leader, can't trust your people, are unable to delegate, then you have not done the right job on yourself and as a result the whole thing will grind inexorably to a halt.

What actually is *relationship*? The dictionary is not too helpful, it defines the noun as

1. The way in which two or more people (or things) are connected, or the state of being connected

2. The way in which two or more people or groups feel about and behave towards each other.

Possibly the second of these is more helpful. "How people feel about and behave towards each other." Can there be anything more important within teams?

Negativity

We have all seen the effect of one negative person in a group. However positive the rest of the team, that one person, like it or not, can bring the whole intent down, can pull the team to failure. That doesn't just mean positive thinking, it means avoiding the effect of negativity on the team, the project and ultimately the success of the company. How do we avoid negativity? How do we ensure that the glass is seen to be half full and not half empty or, as one engineer friend put it to me, the glass is neither half full nor half empty, it has been engineered incorrectly!

My strategy was to wear a thick rubber band around my wrist – the sort the postman drops on the doorstep – and every time I felt a negative thought coming on I would twang the band so that it hurt. After a month or so, I stopped focusing on the negative. Another concept is that we have two dogs, one on each shoulder. One is positive, one negative. Stop feeding the negative dog! The rubber band idea comes from the concept of habit changing. Just repeat something for thirty days or more and it will become a habit. Obviously we need to ensure that we only do good and positive things for each thirty-day period.

One thing I found quite difficult as a CEO was MWBA, management by walking about. I knew it was an essential part of being the boss, I knew that one had to build relationships with one's teams but nevertheless the actual process of walking around and saying something meaningful to a number of people perhaps twice a day, I found hard. I guess that might be part of my make-up just as I found networking a most difficult process. As I mentioned earlier, I put it down to being told never to talk to strangers when I was a child! How on earth did I expect my teams to have any respect for me, to understand what I was getting at in my pronouncements if I hadn't taken the trouble to nurture my relationships with them? OK, I might have found it difficult to relate to outsiders but why on earth was that the case with colleagues, partners, staff? Ah, the benefit of hindsight! So, in a way, this is networking within the team.

The practical aspects

What are the ways we can build these internal relationships? 'Away days', 'family days', reward trips, family rewards, meetings, beer and nibbles, 'employee of the month', mock celebrations. 'Yuck' to all of these if they're not done properly, or are not done with the right motives. There must be a proper system, there must be a positive impetus; the planning must be meticulous and the execution too must be absolutely first class otherwise the whole exercise will be wasted. My own view is that relationships can best be built on a one-to-one basis against a backdrop of formality. In other words, there must be a structured process. Meetings must be properly organised, properly held, with a stated desired outcome and, most importantly, goals, with a planned and timed agenda. Lencioni feels so strongly about this he has published another book, *Death by Meeting*!

Wickman's EOS system (Entrepreneurial Operating System®) is based on a series of structured meetings. It's not just the meeting itself that needs to be structured but the programme of meetings needs to be sacrosanct. Meetings should be regular, set in everyone's calendar and never moved except in very extreme circumstances. This applies to the team meetings for updates and planning, the one-to-one meetings and the quarterly results meetings. It doesn't matter. They should be in the diary even 18 months ahead so that people can plan their business trips and vacations accordingly and well in advance. Sure there will be hiccups but at least all will be aware. It's all part of implementing, building and nurturing relationships. The irony is that against a structured background, companies and teams can still be entrepreneurial and pragmatic.

Couple this with the decision tree explained in Chapter 4, and we will forge a business that knows where it wants to go, knows what it's doing, with people who are all *au fait* with 'the way things are done around here'. Again, that fits in with vision, objectives and values. Relationships will be that much stronger if all is clear and understood. A good way of preparing the ground is for every employee to receive and understand the 'compact'. This is not an employment contract but a short document stating that in addition to pay and rations, the company expects certain things from the employee such as an adherence to the company values and the employee can expect certain things like being treated with respect and understanding and a certain amount of training. Each company should draw up such a compact to suit its own culture and values. This is something that might be difficult to arrange but can provide huge value in the longer term.

Employment law incorporates the concept that discrimination of six types is illegal and can be claimed against by employees. We do need to recognise that while a company may consider itself to be an 'equal-opportunities' employer, either there may be some individuals who have a personal angst towards certain groups – certain ethnicities, certain age groups – which they may hide but which will temper their attitudes towards their fellow employees. This may in itself cause issues to arise which have to be handled with delicacy and care otherwise not only will relationships break down but the outcome could be costly both in time and money trying to repair a situation or, worse, going through a wasteful tribunal process. Recruiting the right people (see next chapter) and training them properly from the start is essential. We thus have to recognise that training does not just cover the skills needed for the execution of the job role itself.

If there is a greater understanding within a company that its employees and its bosses are human beings as well as business people, there will be a much greater chance of success. When I was brought to London to run another broking business, the CEO did not espouse such values. His attitude was that if someone did something right that's what they were paid for. If they did something wrong they should be kicked up and down stairs until they learned. As I mentioned earlier, I was fortunate enough to be fired by him. He was fired by the board a short while later!

Thus it can be seen that relationship and relationships are key aspects of successful business. Without them business will grind to a halt. Be it relationships with those outside the company or those inside, they have to be established, nurtured and, if I can use the word in a positive sense, exploited. Nobel Prize winner, Daniel Kahneman, in his best seller *Thinking, Fast and Slow*, encapsulates much about what we are speaking. Much of relationship comes from the idea of feeling, 'System 1 thinking', the automatic, the intuitive. Thus there is much work to be done if we get a negative feeling at the introduction stage and that is so easy to pick up and to transmit if our attitudes are in any way blocking the process. Get it right, however, and we are able to move forward and be successful, in our endeavours.

Succession planning

Please remember
To identify
Your
Successor;
An essential part
Of running
Your business
An essential part
Of planning
The future of
Your company,
Given
That your desire
Is to build
And have the business
Continue
When you and
Any partners you

May have
Come to the end
Of the useful
Activity
In the business.
Choose a successor
Early on
Not necessarily
With their knowledge
Groom them
And nurture them
As a mentor
So that when it is time
Or when it is that
Runaway bus
Your successor
Is ready to take over
With spirit and with verve

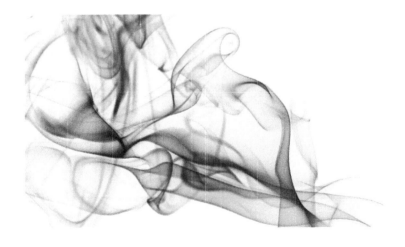

CHAPTER NINE

Succession planning is essential

Your thinking can't start too soon in order to drive yourself in the leadership role.

SUCCESSION PLANNING has been referred to directly and indirectly throughout this book including a reference to my father choosing an outsider to take over from him because he recognised I wasn't minded to do so. This reminds me of the old Jewish Mother (guilt) story. Ben's parents have given him a great education and encouraged him to have a professional career so he works hard, goes to university and eventually becomes a barrister (that's a lawyer not a server in a coffee shop). His mother tells him how proud she and his father are of Ben but can't resist adding that his father is a little disappointed that Ben doesn't want to follow his father into the button business!

Succession planning is essential for a whole host of reasons not least so that the business can continue to grow and prosper and, as we have seen, it's not necessarily because the boss wants to retire or go off and play golf in the sunset. The reasons are manifold. The process is made much easier if the rules of relationship discussed in the previous chapter are followed, the building of both internal and external relationships, as these give rise to a much greater crop of possibilities than otherwise.

Follow-on is essential as it gives an extra dimension to the business building process. If we can see the way over or through the forest we are much more likely to get there than if we just look into it. As the old puzzle goes: "how far into the forest can you walk?" Answer: "half way, because after that you are walking out." So, it follows that looking through to the other side, looking through to what it will be like, helps one to grow, to build and develop one's business.

Of course, things come out of the forest to put obstacles in your way; they could be Alligators, Bears, Crows or even Black Swans. The Black Swans we've already talked about. They are the totally unexpected things that come out of left field – not even out of the forest, if I can be permitted to mix the metaphor even further. How can we expect the unexpected? Of course we can't expect that something unexpected will happen during the lifetime of a business or your lifetime as its leader. It could be a radical change in tax law, it could be the motor accident that changes your life or that of a nearest and dearest or key member of your team. It could be that disruptive product that wipes the floor with yours – consider the Sony Walkman once the iPod came on the market.

Consider what has happened to music and to books – one wonders perhaps why I'm writing one. They (if not this one) will still be read, or listened to, even if the means of reading them is different. In the Age of Aquarius, the Information Age, heralded by that outrageous 1968 musical *Hair*, we have information overload, but one questions whether we have knowledge overload. The key is, of course, turning the information into knowledge, be that in business or elsewhere. By 2025, it is estimated that 75% of the workforce will be Millennials, Generation Y, those born after the mid eighties and into the early part of the 2000s and, as we learnt earlier, they are different – they can use all this stuff – but will they be able to continue and grow your business the way it is today? Clearly not, so in succession planning, we must also ensure that we bring in their thinking as well as that of our contemporaries.

That's what the ABC menagerie, the Alligators, Bears and Crows are in assessing threats. The Alligators are fierce; they are at your heels and with one gnash of fearsome jaws will destroy you. The Bears, although you can see them, are much further away; they are however much faster than you realise and will be upon you before you have time to plan. On the other hand the Crows are those irritants that will peck away at you, gradually wearing you down if you don't do something about them. Occasionally, as in Hitchcock's *Birds* they will turn really vicious.

Business is often referred to as a minefield – clearly it's also a menagerie! Whether it is a minefield or a menagerie, it's not easy. It's hard work even if you enjoy it and of course, as we've said earlier, enjoying the prime purpose of the business is one thing, enjoying all the 'stuff' that goes with it is another. Yet again, choosing a successor earlier rather than later can help you in this arena. By bringing about you the equivalent of a COO (chief operating officer in a larger business or, operations manager in a smaller one) you can delegate all the stuff you don't want to be exercised with so that you can concentrate on that which you are passionate about. So, in this scenario, the successor will manage the business, while you continue to lead and eventually you will find a parallel successor who is as passionate about your product or service as you are. This strategy also allows you to carry on as leader much longer than you would otherwise be able.

Planning the time

Clearly, particularly in a smaller business, this can't be done overnight, it has to be a planned process. However, even if it is expressed as a period of years, it can still be shown as an extended Gantt chart. For those unfamiliar with this terminology, a Gantt chart is a series of bars covering segments of time during which you plan to do things as part of an overall project. It was first developed in the 1910s by Henry Gantt.

Gantt Chart

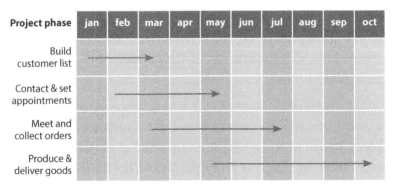

Project phase	jan	feb	mar	apr	may	jun	jul	aug	sep	oct
Build customer list										
Contact & set appointments										
Meet and collect orders										
Produce & deliver goods										

Thus, in a manufacturing business, as a very simplistic example, from January to March you plan to build your list of customers; from February through May, you contact and set appointments; from March through July you meet those potential customers and take orders. From May through to October you produce and deliver the goods. This is shown on a chart without all the words and becomes much clearer, can be seen by everyone involved who can also picture just where they fit in the overall scheme of things.

The second in command

As we can see succession is a vital part of growing your business. There are any number of reasons, beside the unexpected, that point to the essential process of identifying and selecting a successor. We referred to the Charles Handy view that there's no such thing as work/life balance because work is part of life but what we do need to consider is just how much a part of life does work have to be. Yes, there are those who live for their work. We all know coding geeks who love to practise their dark arts half the night but they are probably Millennials who don't necessarily consider coding as work; to them it's play!

However, people grow up, they have relationships outside of work and want to play a little more. You will too once your business has developed and you have a family. In these cases you must find and build your team. Even if you have no intention of selling, retiring, exiting, you do need a second in command, one who could be your successor if anything happened to you or you decide that the time has arrived for you to re-focus or de-focus or possibly, your significant other has made that decision for you or at least planted that idea in your head!

You're successfully building your business. You've got the right people on the bus, to quote Jim Collins again, and you've got them in the right seats. You're getting traction from the flywheel and things are beginning to happen in the way you had hoped. What now? How do you ensure that the momentum will continue with all those outside influences we talked about – and we didn't even mention competitors, suppliers going out of business, major customers going bust? We must have a broader team. It cannot be a 'one man' or 'one woman' show. Even if you have people on the bus, are you the only driver? Is there a conductor? I Is there a ticket inspector? In other words, have you a top team, an SMT, a senior management team to help you run and grow the company? This is all part of succession planning. Succession is not just finding the one person to take over from you when the time comes.

Family businesses: the dangers

Let's take a break and talk about family businesses for a moment. These can be everyone's worst nightmare and I'm not just talking about my first experience with the mynah bird. The problem is that the founder or his (and again, at the moment, it will inevitably have been a male) father or grandfather, usually has fixed ideas about how the company should be run and again inevitably, the son(s) and/or daughter(s) will have different ideas. Compound that with the fact that the elder offspring will usually feel it is their God-given right (OK *primogeniture*) to take over when their parent retires or is playing too much golf or having too many holidays.

It is often the case that the brightest and most able or the most creative is not that eldest child. What then? For this reason, many such businesses, even if the child has gone off to another company to gain experience and/or has gone to business school to earn an MBA, a younger sibling may be a more natural successor. This is very tricky situation and has often caused there to be an unchanged scenario while the parent hopes that it'll all work out in the end. That's why the old saying 'clogs to clogs in three generations' is not just a fanciful issue, it too often comes true and the company folds instead of continuing to grow.

To prevent this, the family should face the facts and be preparing to sell, to bring in outsiders or to make a strategic acquisition. Any one of these can be the route to salvation. In order to help them face the facts, it may be necessary to bring in a third party adviser, non-executive director, or, as I have come across, the parent and/or the child join (separate) advisory groups and work it out with their respective peers. These people may or may not be in a similar position but are able to look at the situation without emotion. Being dispassionate in a passionate environment is not easy for those directly involved, but is often the only way to a sound solution.

Naturally, birth order can play a huge part. I was told the story the other day by the non-executive chairman of a manu-facturing business, where the other directors were four broth-ers, two of whom had not spoken to each other for three years! At board meetings they would sit in regular but distant places.

One day the chairman asked them to sit in birth order so that the two who were not on speaking terms had to sit next to each other. They started talking and didn't stop for 45 minutes. They've been communicating ever since. Whole studies have been done on organisational systems and the influence of past events on the present and the future. For those interested in reading further take a look at the controversial 'Constellations' work of German, Bert Hellinger. In a quick study Wikipedia reports that some say it's mumbo jumbo; others swear that it is a really powerful therapeutic method.

Another strategy is to branch out. Give one or more of the offspring the opportunity to set up and run their own businesses, which can be funded partly by the parent company. This way each of them is being given their head and, if successful, will bring new fortunes to the family firm. The better way is for each of the new businesses to be allied to the first so that there will be synergy, there will be an opportunity to grow the equivalent of divisions and thus ensure that each part 'sticks to its knitting' and prospers instead of the original company failing because it has diversified too much. If successful, the family group of companies could be a really valuable prize for a buyer either in whole or in part. A very public example of this is the now hugely successful jewellery arm of the crystal glass Swarovski business, conceived and developed by Nadja Swarovski, a great, great, granddaughter of the founder.

An alternative would be to go out and buy another business for one of the family to run. Care must be taken here because of differing cultures, which may or may not allow full alignment. Differing cultures is the reason 70% of mergers fail according to KPMG research. However, as we've already shown, cultures and values within one business can be different particularly when it comes to family concerns. So much for the family business. I'm not saying that all fail. What I am saying is that when it comes to succession it is, ironically, often more difficult for family businesses than we might expect to be the case.

All businesses

We were talking about the SMT, the senior management team. Is it always the case that this will contain the successor? Not necessarily; it may not even contain anyone who has the remotest interest in being the next leader. However, in my view all should have the capability of so being. As Wickman asks, "do they get it, want it and have they the capacity to do it?" We must check, we must verify, we must ensure that our SMT is made up of people who have those characteristics. The capability can, in some cases, be trained. However, they must 'get it'; in other words, they must understand what it's all about and they must 'want it' otherwise they'll just be marking time until they find what they really want to do. That is the best way to extreme self-demotivation; just having a job and as somebody once said having a 'job' is J.O.B. 'just over broke'. It's a stepping stone to nowhere.

What if someone in the team does want to de-focus, do something else, be somewhere else? It might even be the boss who wants fresh pastures. There needs to be a development plan in every business to ensure that there are successors, people ready to jump into others' shoes but at the same time we can't risk real de-motivation by allowing people to think that the only way to promotion is the possibility of someone deciding to leave. We have to build a company where there are true career development opportunities. We identified earlier that Gen Y and Millennials will usually not be happy staying in one place 'for life'. There's too much going on out there. They're too ambitious to want to map out their whole career once they've left university and have started their first job since graduating. They won't use a Gantt chart to look to the end of their days in business. There's no longer such thing as working and looking forward to retirement at 60 or 65. If anything they will be looking to have made their fortune by 50 or 55 and, so a very brief window indeed where there is stability for the employer.

The employer, the boss, has to have a different attitude than that of their forbears. It's a different challenge, a different scenario and not just for planning purposes. It makes for a complex infrastructure on which to base your business. Tempered only by recent recessionary times, employees will always be restless so we're back to motivation, retention, encouragement and what better encouragement, what better motivation than the thought of being a part owner. It does surprise me that more owners don't believe in the concept of giving some equity to their people, as with the John Lewis concept of making all staff 'partners'. Mark Fritz, who we mentioned in Chapter 4, avers that unless you actually own something you don't value it. So, in business, the idea is that, even if it is only phantom equity rather than voting shares, the employee will feel like an owner, will take more pride in growing the business, feeling that they will benefit financially when the company is sold or passed on. Owners should not consider the sharing of equity as giving it away. A smaller part of a bigger cake is often more valuable than the whole cake particularly if, by making these arrangements, the company grows bigger faster.

A word of caution here: I've seen too many cases where a boss has promised equity or equity equivalent but greed or inertia or just procrastination has prevented this happening. This is not only demotivating, it destroys trust within the company and we have seen how important trust is in making a company grow and prosper.

Mergers and acquisitions

In talking about succession, we need to consider the sale of the company, which is one way of ensuring succession. We also need to look at acquisition be it acquiring for diversification or acquiring a company to allow that company's boss to be your successor.

As a former corporate financier, I have seen good sales and bad sales. The key is to plan and to prepare. Again it's a matter of vision. It's seeing how you want the future to pan out and then planning for it. Again my overriding view is that we need to share that vision with the team and we need to ensure that they are just as motivated to get there as we are. It's no good keeping things a secret. My rule of thumb, proven time after time, is that if there's something to be found out it will be. The FT agreed with me when they published my letter on this point following a series of so-called 'leaks' from the cabinet office. More recently we've seen WikiLeaks. When I was a child I was told to be careful what I said on the phone as you 'never knew who was listening'! That was in the days of telephone operators and well before phone hacking.

As a former chairman of the Manchester Stock Exchange, I was involved in talks with other broking firms about the possibility of forming a trade association to further the interests of broking firms all over the UK. At the time Henry

Cooke had an office in Leeds following its acquisition of local firm Howitt and Pemberton. I used to go there once or twice a month. I used one such opportunity to visit a competitor in Huddersfield to discuss with their CEO the possibility of him taking part and indeed becoming a member. By the time I got back to Manchester, the story was all round the office, and indeed the town, that our two firms were about to merge! That was in the early days of APCIMS, the Association of Private Client Investment Managers and Stockbrokers.

On another occasion, I was told by a member of staff that we were merging with a Midlands firm. Each firm had sworn the other to secrecy; we had code names for code names. It was still 'fact' although we never did merge! Ever since, I have worked on the principle that a cover story is not enough and that applies whether you are the protagonist or the adviser. You must plan for this eventuality. And, however you plan it, a Black Swan is likely to appear and upset things for you.

In the public arena we see this time after time. It happens. We need to accept the fact. Of course, in the marketplace trading on such information is now illegal. I do remember a Chinese client once telling me that he thought it pointless buying shares unless he had inside information. Perhaps he had a valid point!

The nub is, that for whatever reason you plan a merger or acquisition, you need to make sure your team is involved. This needs to be agreed with your target company otherwise Murphy's Law will take over and what can go wrong will go wrong. The point we're still labouring here is your succession plan. The same applies to outright sale where you want to exit, preferably for 'loadsamoney'. Whether it's an outright sale, a leveraged buyout, a merger, or an earn-out, all need to be planned meticulously. Whatever the vehicle and whatever the prime reason, it's no good hoping for the best. Yes, I know that advisers and corporate financiers (and one of the best in the business is the aforementioned Jo Haigh) are expensive but when you weigh up what they can do for you, in terms of achieving the desired result and the anguish they can save you, they are worth every penny. I'm not talking my own book here, as I stopped being in that business a long time ago but I do have a special, if not unique, perspective on the process.

Sale of the business

This chapter is primarily about succession planning so let's look at a sale in that context. In just the same way as you plan to find a particular individual to be your successor, there are different ways of achieving that end. You could buy a company because it has a great leader (in your opinion) but would that individual still be a great leader in your business? You need to look at how they have built their business. Are the ethics the same, are the ethos and the values and the culture similar? They won't be identical but they could be programmed to ensure that in due course there is one culture, one set of values. Despite the KPMG research, there have been some extraordinarily successful deals where companies have got together and produced fine results. I don't think they happen without meticulous due diligence and planning. Is it the equivalent of a sledgehammer to crack a nut? Possibly, but if it's necessary to get the right people on your bus then so be it. The acquirer will need to consider this very carefully.

We have seen a number of cases where such strategy is considered a stepping stone. There is an interim situation where the two bosses become joint CEOs. Disaster – there can be only one boss, period. By all means one becomes CEO, the other chairperson, but that chairperson must not in any circumstances be an executive chairperson. Of course, there's no distinction in company law between executive and non-executive, but it can be the road to extinction if there is not one final arbiter.

The board of directors

That leads to another point; too many companies, particularly growing SMEs, don't really understand the purpose and the powers and duties of the board. Jo has written a great book *The Business Rules*, which is well worth reading on the subject. The chair runs the board which, in turn, agrees the strategy put forward by the CEO and the senior management team and delegates the execution of the strategy to that *executive* team. True, in smaller companies, non-executives can bring particular knowledge, connections and experience to be shared with the executive team but they shouldn't be doing their job. As far as large corporate entities are concerned, my belief is that to be truly independent, as required by the regulators, non-executives should not be former executives in that particular business otherwise the tendency is for them to 'go native' or to believe the team should be acting in the business the way they did, oblivious to the fact that times change and are, as we've already discussed, changing faster than ever. As Marshall Goldsmith says, "What got you here, won't get you there."

The planning process for sale

The planning cannot start too soon. Well, perhaps that's a bit too much of a sweeping statement. Just as we should plan to be replaced by our successor very early on in the history of our tenure, so we should be planning an exit as soon as we decide that's the way we would like to go. It seems obvious if the vision is to launch, build and ultimately sell a business. Thus, we see another point in favour of a well thought out vision and plan to achieve that vision. However, even if it isn't quite as well formulated, it seems to make sense to view the uplands from the valley, take the longer view and have it in mind when working out the steps you need to take. If we do that we're much more likely to get where we want to go. It's no good, as the old Irish story has it, that we 'shouldn't start from here', and (back to Alice again) it doesn't matter how you do it – blue sky thinking, brainstorming, six thinking hats, tossing a coin – the important thing is that you make a decision, you pursue that decision, you ensure that you have the right team about you and, I'll repeat, I don't believe you'll get where you want to get unless they are in your confidence. Back to trust again.

So, draw up what the organogram will need to look like and try and fill the slots as time progresses, ever bearing in mind that until sales and resources allow, watching margins, break-even and the like, you must ensure that you are not over trading, are not running a cash poor operation, are not running out of steam and proceeding to insolvency rather than success. No, running a business, building a business, is not easy, unless you happen to be a fourteen-year-old geek who produces the killer App and gets bought out for few handy million by Facebook or Google. They hit the headlines but there aren't that many of them. Despite social media, it's still a bit of a slog!

How do we find the right buyer, or for that matter, the right target to acquire? There are a number of agencies who can help. These tend to be the corporate finance boutiques as we're predominantly speaking about SMEs, rather than larger companies. They see buyers and sellers all the time and are probably best positioned to find the right partners for your business. Again, they're running their own businesses and make their money by putting deals together so they are not altogether altruistic in wanting a particular deal to happen.

However, try to position your company as one that is special, one that, if bought by the other, will transform their business. As a result they'll probably be prepared to pay far more than market price. On the other hand, if you're the buyer try and spot a target that could do the same for you. Of course they and their advisers will be on the look out to see that they're not being exploited. It's a merger of interests (yes, I know there's no such thing as a true merger – there will always be one buying and one selling, one in charge and one subordinate) but here I'm talking about merging the underlying businesses in order to become more powerful in the marketplace rather than the actual company position. Again it's a matter of perspective.

Much better to have the plan there for the future than trying to execute when you feel that you MUST take action, that you need to take action rather than when you want to take action. We talked about the difference between needs and wants in an earlier chapter – the difference between wanting a drink and needing a drink. Yes, a bit banal when talking about wanting to buy a company, wanting to sell a company. Much better than needing to take either action. Be in control. That way it's much easier to play to win. You go to the ironmongers because you need a drill. No, you want a drill because you need a six-inch hole in the wall!

There are a number of reasons why we need to build good business relationships as we outlined in the previous chapter.

Another is to spot the potential buyer or potential to be bought, even if they are competitors at the early stage. Talk to your competitors. First, it can disarm them, second, you may learn something you don't know about your marketplace, third, you may find a willingness to enter into a joint venture, where you can both benefit. However, care is needed here, as John Kay, the FT columnist, wrote, you must set it up properly otherwise what often happens is that both parties will think the other is providing the particular input, which is just not happening. Also remember that other companies may not be providing the same product or service as yours but their market is the same, particularly if aimed at the consumer who can afford or finds an appeal in only one of the two offerings. So, my view is talk to them too. You may find that by working together there is a synergy that gives rise to something more in due time.

What I've tried to show in this chapter is that there's more to succession planning than just finding an individual within or without the company to become your successor. There are several ways and not all are mutually exclusive. You may find that a purchase brings with it the right person to take over your position. Alternatively, you may have spotted someone in the marketplace who would be ideal to bring your company and someone else's together, but would not necessarily be happy just to come to you; someone who needs a greater challenge to create that synergy that we're all searching for. Be open to fresh ideas; be on the lookout for opportunities that may otherwise pass you by. Business is not just about being busy, to make a rather trite comment. However, just how many businesses do we come across where the day-to-day objective or *de facto* situation is, as someone once put it, being 'busy fools'?

Recruitment

Do not forever
Recruit
In your own
Image.
Learn to identify
The now needs
And the future needs
Of the business,
The traits necessary
The traits essential
The traits that are key
To the success
You seek to lead
That you seek
To achieve
That you seek
To accomplish
When leading
When growing

When designing
The needs to arrive
At your vision
To arrive
At your destination.
Ensure that
You have
'The right people
On
The bus' (although
A different bus than
That which has a tendency
To mow many
Down
On its errant way
To its own
Destination
In town!)

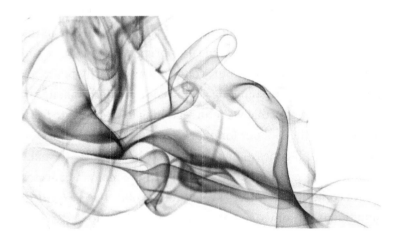

CHAPTER TEN

Recruitment - hire slow, fire fast

Getting the right people on board.

WE'VE TALKED about making sure that you have the right people in your team, about building for succession. So why do we need a whole chapter on the subject of recruitment? Because, in my view, this is one of the worst aspects of the way smaller businesses are run. We are often so desperate to find someone to do the job, to fill a gap to make more sales, that the process we go through is extraordinarily lacking from both a scientific and a creative point of view. We've said before, 'hire slow, fire fast'. Sure, there are employment laws that get in the way of the latter, particularly in the UK, but these laws have sensibly been modified in recent times. True they are not as free-spirited as those in the US but eminently more flexible than they are in France and Italy.

As far as hiring is concerned, just look at the cost of a bad hire even ignoring the cost of recruitment fees. If you employ someone for a £50k-a-year job, that's probably £60k with National Insurance and office costs and if it's pensionable you can add even more. You don't take on new staff with a view to employing them for less than say, five years, so that's a £300,000 investment. You will certainly agonise for much, much, longer before spending a fraction of that on some new furniture or cars or decor. Why not agonise for longer on bringing in someone who hopefully will generate maybe three to four times their costs in revenue terms, so this project is worth well over a £1,000,000 to the company if we get it right. If we get it wrong, we lose maybe six months to a year before a replacement begins to generate the right sort of return, so it is essential to get the recruitment right, to recruit the right people from the start.

Interviews follow the same routine. Someone comes through the door, they 'look right' they come over with confidence and seem to answer our simple questions with alacrity and, as I've said, we're so desperate to recruit that we not only want to hire them on the spot, we spend most of the interview telling them what a wonderful company we have and why they should be so pleased to work here. This has to be nonsense. Probably equal nonsense is the 'Microsoft' question. I'm not sure whether these are still used but there's even a book on the subject *How Would You Move Mount Fuji?* that includes questions such as "Why are manholes round?" We're not operating an entrance interview for Oxbridge. We have serious need and, as suggested by Wickman, they've got to 'get it', 'want it', 'have the capacity to do it'. So the interview must be conducted to find out these things. What have they done before, in terms of achievements? How did they tackle a particular issue? What happened? What was the impact on their peers? It's a provocative subject; in a recent article, Lucy Kellaway even suggested using an online dating site might be a great way of avoiding all the time and expense of finding the right people.

One of the key tools that I learned to use was the 'Glossary of Traits' put together by former Vistage speaker, Ed Ryan. This is reproduced here. We need to examine motivations, modes of thinking, modes of acting and modes of interacting. The overriding instruction is to ensure that you select at least one of the *Motivations* traits and rate it as #1 Critical. The motivation traits do show up the candidate as to where their drive comes from and what provides fulfilment particularly in their work activity. It has to stand out as being much more than the simple desire to earn money to satisfy basic necessities.

GLOSSARY of TRAITS – Source Ed Ryan
Ensure that you select at least one of the MOTIVATIONS TRAITS and rate it as (1) <u>Critical</u>

MOTIVATIONS	Behavioral traits that address the fundamental "drives" of an individual and are characterized by more than the simple desire to earn money to satisfy basic necessities; that is, what provides the individual with fulfillment through work activities. (At least one of these 6 traits must be selected as critical)		
ACHIEVER (Individual)	• Confident and Self-assured • Seeks independence and recognition • Driven to high levels of accomplishment		
COMPETITOR (Individual)	• Energized by competition • Responds to measurable performed goals • Driven to produce		
MISSION OF SERVICE (Individual & Management)	• Service oriented • Team player • Committed to family and community		
PRODUCER (Management)	• Results oriented • Seeks objectives • Measures performance throughout the unit		
RESPONSIBILITY (Individual)	• Conscientious and dependable • Good attendance and punctuality • Committed to delivery of tasks		
TECHNICAL MASTERY (Individual) (For technical positions only)	• Committed to continual self-education • Large store of industry knowledge • Intrigued by new developments		

MODES of THINKING	Behaviors that address an individual's capacity to gather information and process it (sort, parse, problem-solve & analyze). Additionally, it looks at an individual's ethical principles, as well as, their creativity, flexibility, and adaptability.	
DECISION MAKER (Management)	• Thorough research • Aware of parts-to-whole relationship • Strives to harmonize competing interests	
DISCERNER (Individual)	• Skilled in self-appraisal • Quickly sorts the critical from the superfluous • Acts appropriately	
INNOVATOR (Individual & Management)	• Constant search for better methods • Flexible and adaptive • Encourages new ideas	
VALUES (Individual)	• Integrity and honesty are hallmarks • Refuses to cut corners or over-promise • Represents company judiciously	
MODES of ACTING	Behavioral traits that address an individual's approach and skills for accomplishing work functions. These would include organizational and time management skills, planning and prioritization, as well as, initiative, work focus and physical and mental stamina. These are essentially job related, functional traits.	
ARRANGER (Management)	• Deploys resources effectively • Concerned with efficiency and streamlining • Long range planner	
CULTIVATOR (Management)	• Forward looking • Aware of company position in the market place • Quality conscious	

MODES of THINKING Cont'd	Behaviors that address an individual's capacity to gather information and process it (sort, parse, problem-solve & analyze). Additionally, it looks at an individual's ethical principles, as well as, their creativity, flexibility, and adaptability.			
DEVELOPER (Management)	• Astute selection decisions • Personal attention to training & coaching • Sense of satisfaction in growth of subsidiaries			
INTENSITY (Individual)	• High stamina & endurance • Focus on work activities • Active hobbies			
PROACTIVITY (Individual)	• Looks for solutions • Initiates change & improvement • Doesn't blame or shirk responsibility			
PROSPECTOR (Individual Sales)	• Targets accounts carefully • Continually probe & penetrate accounts • Methodical assessment of "fit" between prospect & the company			
RESEARCHER (Individual technical & systems)	• Full range of information gathering techniques • Methodical hypothesis formation and testing • Skilled troubleshooter			
STRATEGIST (Individual)	• Well organized and skilled in prioritizing • Well developed grand planning skills • Brings tasks to closure			
TECHNICAL MASTERY (Individual) (For non-technical positions only)	• Committed to continual self-education • Large store of industry knowledge • Intrigued by new developments			

MODES of INTERACTING	Behaviors that address an individual's inter-personal skills, that is, how they influence, interact, and get along with others.		
AFFILIATIONS (Individual Technical & Systems)	• Enjoys sharing expertise with other professionals • Contributes to team bonding • Taps into knowledge in a variety of fields		
ASSERTOR (Individual)	• Straightforward & direct • Opens doors, closes deals • Sense of drive and aggressiveness		
COMMUNICATOR (Individual)	• Adapts to level and interest of others • Confident public speaker • Articulate conversationalist		
EMPATHY (Individual)	• Sensitive listener • Recognizes role of human nature in business decisions • Need to reach out and comfort		
MOTIVATOR (Management)	• Stimulates enthusiasm • Creates 'buy-in' from employees • Utilizes incentives and praise generously		
PERSUADER (Individual)	• Skilled listener who identifies motivations • Probes and questions others' agendas • Strives to influence others		
RELATOR (Individual & Management)	• Outgoing & congenial • Takes time to engage associates on a personal level • Promotes harmony and positive relationships		

OK, lots of traits. How do we choose the ones we really, really need? This is where we must analyse the job role and person spec. Too often have we seen the recruiter or their agent just choose someone because they're available and not because they are the right person for the role. In a growing business as well as in a formative one it is absolutely essential that the job role is thoroughly identified, that the characteristics required are painstakingly thought out. Yes, we know a sales person must sell but what, how, when, why are still only four questions to be answered. I'd also like to know to whom and where? I'd like to know precisely what traits they should have for the role, for their place in the team, for the product or service we have to sell, wherever they are in the organisation. It's my view, and this fits in with what was said about vision, even if you're not actually employed for business development, you need to know what the business is all about, what it can do for the customer and therefore what is its likely future.

I've not covered psychometrics and the many models thereof, Belbin, Myers Briggs, DISC. I don't believe that they should be consigned to the laughter zone. After all, the first time I was subjected to one of these tests – I'm not sure which one – in six minutes, I'd given away such a huge amount about myself that I vowed never to allow myself to be importuned in this way again! As a support for a recruitment operation, they can provide some helpful perspectives but they should never be used in isolation.

Of course, a vital aspect is that of leadership. The traits described above refer to recruits as individuals and sometimes as individuals and managers. We must also look at the qualities of our teams in terms of leadership. I like this comparison of leaders and managers:

Managers	Leaders
• The manager administers	• The leader innovates
• The manager is a copy	• The leader is an original
• The manager maintains	• The leader develops
• The manager focuses on systems and structure	• The leader focuses on people
• The manager relies on control	• The leader inspires trust
• The manager has a short range view	• The leader has a long range perspective
• The manager asks how and when	• The leader asks what and why
• The manager has his/her eye always on the bottom line	• The leader has his/her eye on the horizon
• The manager initiates	
• The manager accepts the status quo	• The leader originates
	• The leader challenges it
• The manager is a classic good soldier	• The leader is his own person
The manager does things right	**The leader does the right thing**

Yes, a few clichés there, but still apposite and worthy of note. Also, as John Quincy Adams, sixth President of the US from 1825 to 1829 (b.1767–d.1848) said, "If your actions inspire others to dream more, learn more, do more and become more, you are a leader."

Using these tools is using both left and right brain, looking at the words, looking at the numbers and asking the right questions. Many of the questions can in the first instance be asked, for a price, by agents, recruiters, career specialists. There is at least one organisation that trains people with aptitude to be focused sales people in the technology arena. They focus on aptitude first and they test that attribute before spending time on development and putting people into the marketplace. To my mind that is money well spent. Brian M took on such a young person for his European businesses, who was such a star that he asked her to help him open up in China.

Recruiters cost money, so do other means of attracting the right people. An American law firm here in London, will pay its staff £10,000 if they introduce good new associates, who last a probationary period. Some companies will pay £1,000, which they may feel sounds a lot in isolation but set against the expected return, it really is derisory. Think about it. Feel how you would feel! Return on investment must be both concrete and feel right to be truly effective. Networking, though, as we've talked about before, can also be a great way of finding the right people. Empower your team to find the right people through networking. After all they're likely to meet the sort of people you're looking for and who they'll be able to get on with and thus help each other generate the right results. So, another very valuable use of networking, something we must constantly bear in mind.

The recruit's perspective

Let's look at recruitment from the new employee's point of view for a moment. If we get it wrong, they can suffer enormously. It's so important that we get the right people for their own good or again, they'll be such misfits that they can do terrible damage to the company. I've seen examples of perceived bullying, discrimination and so forth just because the employee needs to latch on to an injustice that may or may not have happened, may or may not be true. Tribunals can be avoided if due process is followed but please, not just slavishly. Set up your processes to take into account the foibles of individuals and ensure that you are able to follow those processes properly. Remember, there are unscrupulous employees who will try to take you to the cleaners not just because they want to generate cash for themselves but because they've been recruited into a place that is just not for them. That is as much your fault as theirs. The fact that there are fewer jobs for people to chase than perhaps there used to be does not make things any easier in this respect. While business generally avoids union members, I have seen cases where staff members join a union just for this type of eventuality. The unions love to represent individuals against businesses.

We've said any number of times that we must get the right people on the bus but how many times have we thought we've done that, only to be proven wrong. Apart from space and money, people are the biggest issue for any business. They may be well-trained, experts in their own field but they are, just like their bosses, human beings. They have similar faults, foibles, irritants, passions, predilections, habits that get in the way of a streamlined business. On any risk register, that must be one of the highest risks! I've not yet seen it mentioned.

On the bright side, well-led, well-motivated, well-remunerated employees, who are encouraged to share the vision, to help engender the mission, will help you ensure that the team play full out for everyone's benefit. Just as we described, though, one negative person pulling down the whole atmosphere in a room, just one disaffected employee, can be a huge danger to a company's wellbeing and prosperity. For larger companies, the UK Corporate Governance Code enshrines 'tone from the top'. In other words the CEO must set an example and ensure that reputation, behaviour and similar concerns are on their agenda in addition to financial performance and results. A survey undertaken by Harvard Business School seems to suggest that only about five CEOs in the top 100 have this cracked. One man comes out top, Jeff Bezos of Amazon. Yet stories abound of the miseries of Amazon employees in their vast warehouses walking up to 15 miles a day! There do not seem to be any rules for smaller companies where the 'tone from the top' will be easier to cascade but may be entirely unsuited to the type of organisation or to its needs.

Be sure that people mean what they say. How often do people in the office think one thing and say another? How many times in teams in the office do you detect that people are sitting round the table thinking one thing and saying another. The great thing about the poetry exercises in Chapter 12 is that once we've opened up like this there's no going back. We can and will be much more open and honest with each other. I find this a useful tool to actually get the truth out of people, it has real meaning. Watch out for examples of group think.

Some time ago, I picked up something called the Abilene paradox, group think in the family situation. Abilene is a place in west central Texas. The father of the family, who is quite stern, says, "we're not doing much today as a family, why don't we go to Abilene? I'm told it's a nice place." "Yeah it will be a nice day out." So they drive for hours and hours – mother, father, grandma and the kids. And they eventually get to Abilene and it's hot and it's dusty and suddenly someone (probably mother) asks "why on earth did we come down here?" "We all wanted to come." "No one wanted to come." "But we wanted to come, we all agreed." But no one agreed, they just went along with the idea.

Mastermind Group

Think
And
Grow Rich
Said
Napoleon Hill
Many, many years ago when
He recommended
The mastermind group
Real or
Virtual
Although
In those days
Virtuality seemed
To mean other
Things.
Today we capture
Ideas, thoughts and
Issues
In a mentally

Stimulating forum
To help achieve
The success
We all yearn
We all desire.
The help of others
Is a wondrous
Thing
Especially when we
Can do the same
For them.
Learn together
Work together
Challenge and
Focus
Together.
Togetherness
In a business
Oriented way.

CHAPTER ELEVEN

Joining and using a mastermind group

The power of working with others in a peer group, both virtual and real, for ultimate support.

IN 1936, NAPOLEON Hill first published *Think and Grow Rich*. Even though that is now nearly eighty years ago, I still recommend it be read by clients and others. It is a seminal work and although many, many, other works have reached our bookshelves, the kernel of this one, the very essence of its ideas, remains of huge value today as it did then. The core concept is that of the mastermind group, which we sometimes refer to as a think tank or as a peer group. It matters not what it is called; it is the central purpose and the ensuing results that matter.

It is recommended that everyone, be they in business or not, get around them a group of individuals who have no vested interest in the individual other than his or her success. The other, perhaps shocking, thing is that these people need not be alive. Or they can be alive but not actually in the room! We can create a virtual group with our imagination. Why? Because when we question them, they respond in our ear, in our consciousness with the most germane and helpful advice. They are true mentors. I can hear you asking just how does this happen? How on earth can it be effective?

Before going into greater detail about the virtual group, let us first take a look at a living and present group of such people and see why their presence can help us. In business and in life, everyone around us has an agenda, has a way of looking at situations, has a way of telling each other what to do. The essence of the mastermind group is that the only agenda on which they are focused is yours. That is the one simple rule. We know that in business as in life, your agenda is yours. Everyone who comes to you either as a direct report, a chair of the board, a significant other in the domestic environment, a member of staff, has something on their mind and it's rarely what you have on yours!

Thus, the senior manager who reports to you as leader is concerned about their problems, their staff, their customers and wants your advice. The chair of the board has a responsibility to see that the board's strategic plans are complied with and executed. The significant other always wants what's good for the two of you or just themselves rather than you in particular. Perhaps I'm being a bit cynical here and over simplifying matters but these latter comments are made by way of illustration and explanation rather than as an unqualified thesis. Therefore, if that is the case, we need to have somewhere to go to consult, almost akin to the Delphic oracle, in order to be able to obtain true unsullied advice that we can act upon without fear of conflict. Although some conflict is good according to Patrick Lencioni (*q.v.*) as long as it is, in his words, 'productive conflict' which ends in agreement and a plan of action duly executed by those empowered to do so.

So, how does the mastermind group work in practice? You, as leader in your business have an issue you wish to resolve. Let us say it's about utilisation of resources. Your business has a limited budget and you need to increase the payroll to recruit someone to help with business development. What do you do to ensure that you take the course of action that best suits the business at this time?

Stage 1: The group will be given an outline of the issue and its importance to the company including, if at all possible, a financial outcome, or value to the resolution of the issue.

Stage 2: Group members ask clarifying questions and the group leader ensures that at this stage, no one is allowed to give a solution disguised as a question such as 'have you thought of...?' So, no leading questions. Clarification means just that, such as what is your employee budget, what proportion of your overheads does that represent? What's more important, marketing or sales? The issue holder will respond briefly and succinctly, so that those sitting around the table will be able to build up a comprehensive picture of the problem for which an answer is being sought. Clearly, if this group meets on a regular basis it will have a substantial insight into how the company and its management team works. So, another benefit of meeting with such a group on a regular basis is one of continuity of thought. The questioning can go on until exhausted or the time limit set by the group leader. Questions can be asked in series or on a 'piggy-back' basis (in series) according to need.

Stage 3: Following the questioning, someone summarises the issue. Quite often, the original issue is not the real issue or problem to be solved. Something else has been overlooked or perhaps hidden and will be brought out by the questioning process. Once that has been done and the issue holder has confirmed that the group is indeed looking at the right issue, the group will offer its advice at stage 4.

Stage 4; This may take the form of straightforward advice as to actions but it can also encompass the expression of some concerns, identification of threats or, on the other hand, identification of opportunities.

Stage 5: Once all have offered their thoughts, the incumbent should take a few moments to cogitate – it never ceases to amaze me how people more often than not want to rush in without prior thought; but on the other hand, because the rule is that the incumbent must keep absolutely quiet during the advice part of the process, the response 'we tried that and it doesn't work' is totally avoided.

To be really effective, whatever the issue holder says they will do following the advice, there must be accountability to the group. They will be told that a report will be given or sent to them by a certain time. The concept of accountability is very powerful and produces a very elemental focus on achieving the desired result.

The virtual group

What, however, is the purpose and composition of a virtual group? We each of us have souls and living persons whom we admire and from whom any advice would be valuable. With living people we have a current view of what they would say if asked for help. That is true whether we know them personally or not, whether we have met them or not. With dead people, we have either experienced their thoughts during their lifetimes or alternatively, we have read or heard so much about them that we feel we would know what they'd have to say if only we'd asked them.

My personal virtual mastermind group is drawn from the following people. I don't necessarily 'ask them' all to every session. Sometimes I might just focus on one in my head at a specific time. They are drawn from the following:

- *My late father*
- *Abraham Lincoln*
- *Genghis Khan – because he formed a nation from a rabble*
- *Attila the Hun – a really process-driven individual*
- *Lucretia Borgia – a very powerful woman*
- *Moses*

The living and very alive:

- *Luke Johnson* – *serial entrepreneur, although I don't always agree with what he says in his FT columns!*

- *Rupert Clevely* – *former member of one of my business peer groups. Built a business from scratch and sold well; a very interesting study (see later in this chapter).*

- *Ivan Goldberg* – *my former chair when I was a member of a peer group as CEO of Henry Cooke Lumsden*

- *Lucy Kellaway* – *of the Financial Times (my favourite columnist). When I told her of her inclusion on the list she asked if there was a fee – of course but it is virtual!*

I do wish I had thought of this concept when a CEO myself. While we had grown the company from partnership to PLC, and our business was to give advice, more outside advisers, other than just our auditors, lawyers and tax advisers would have been, I'm sure, highly beneficial.

Like many people, I use my gut, my intuition, the 'will' as described previously. It is a huge advantage to be able to 'call' on these people to test whether my gut is telling me the right things to do. It usually is but to get a different perspective without leaving one's chair or sometimes one's bed, is, I believe, a huge advantage. Lucretia Borgia and several others were really questioning when it came to writing this book. Some just asked "why?" and I had to come up with a series of reasons. However, it was my mentor who asked me the most difficult question, "just who are you writing it for?" My first answer was, "anyone who'll read it." The focused answer is those who will benefit from reading about my experiences and the experiences of my clients and contacts in the business world. I believe that those who will most benefit are those for whom my words raise a few 'aha's!', if not the occasional epiphany.

As one speaker, Reg Athwal, puts it, "it's for the BIRDS":

Breakthroughs

+ Ideas

+ Remembrances

+ Decisions

= Success

Live mastermind groups

Vistage is one super example of live mastermind groups; private advisory groups for MDs, executives and business owners, peer groups whose mission is "dedicated to increasing the effectiveness and enhancing the lives of chief executives". There are quite a few similar organisations including ACE, The Academy for Chief Executives, YPO/ YEO, Young Presidents/Entrepreneurs Organisation, TAB, the Alternative Board, MD2MD. All have similar aims but work to slightly different models.

The mechanics of Vistage membership are quite simple. Members leave their business premises and connections to spend a day each month with their peer group. That day mostly comprises a morning with a resource speaker, such as the ones I've mentioned. They don't just listen, they take part in an interactive workshop with actions to accomplish when returning to base.

To declare an interest, or in fact several interests, I have been a member of and am a chair of two such groups and a speaker to groups in the UK and in the US. Thus, I do have a number of perspectives on how successful these groups can be. Group chairs generally recruit their own group members, thus, the ethos of each group tends to reflect the chair's predilections. As a speaker, I see many groups and thus see many different ways the facilitator/chair/coach goes about their business. Some are extraordinarily left brained, running their groups to a strict timetable and structure and woe betide any member or guest who strays. On the other hand, I rejoice in my experience of one sadly deceased chair, Armon Kamesar, in La Jolla, California, who rolled up half an hour late and said, "OK what are we doing this morning?" quite forgetting why I had joined them. Perhaps, as my forte as a speaker is how to use the whole brain, neither only 'right' nor only 'left', I'm somewhere between the two extremes. I'm rarely asked for more structure, although sometimes for more strictness on accountability.

MAGIC

The overall benefit of membership can be encapsulated by the mnemonic, MAGIC. There is indeed a magic in being a member.

Making better decisions - for themselves and their companies.

Accountability is one of the key aspects of the groups. Without it the whole exercise can be a waste of time. The things we focus on enabling members to achieve are:

Growth of their companies and themselves

Overcoming the *Isolation* of being in the hot seat

And, *Change.*

In addition to the speakers already referred to there is a large bank of resource speakers who will work with groups on topics as diverse as Stress and Personal Wellbeing to Strategy, Marketing, Sales, Financial Management; indeed, virtually any topic that the chair and the members feel a need to pursue. In the afternoon, issues such as the ones outlined above are processed. Reports on previous issues are also given and often challenged. In between the monthly meeting, the member and chair interact at a two-hour, one to one coaching session. Thus it can be seen that membership is a fairly intensive programme. The key, however, is the ability to be away from the coalface, to take part in strategic thinking, leaving the tactical behind.

For business owners and leaders to invest 5% of their time, it is evident how valuable membership is and how satisfactory the ROI. Dun and Bradstreet, the business information company, in its research found that companies grow two to three times as fast when their leaders are members of this organisation.

Let us take a look at some member successes. As mentioned earlier, companies are of all shapes and sizes. While the general focus is on SMEs there are some groups with members from large corporates. One thing is essential – there are no competitors and no supply chains, so the meeting room is a very safe space for absolutely confidential interchange.

Rupert C had started a tiny pub company with his wife; he had previously been marketing manager for a leading champagne brand. Their concept was, at the time, something relatively new, the gastro-pub. They started with five and gradually built the company with the help of private equity backers to thirty-two, when they were able to sell on very favourable terms to a leading listed brewer and pub owner. Apart from getting the finances right, they learned among other things about leadership versus management, equity funding and business development.

Another individual, Nigel B, joined a group about the same time as Rupert. At the time he was running a TOC, train-operating company, for the very special train used in the Harry Potter films. His boss, owner of an air conditioning business, had been and still is a member of another group. Nigel, after discussions, realised that there was an opening in rolling stock certification and effected a BIMBO (buy-in, management buyout) obtaining control of a small division of a major international engineering company. After growing that business for several years with the support of his peers through some tricky ownership and management concerns, he was able to sell to a large Swiss conglomerate and become global business development officer for their then new train division.

Not everyone enjoys unbridled success. One group member, Luis D, a provider of equipment for bookings in restaurants, banks and legal firms, after expansion into North America, was due to sign up Lehman Brothers on the very morning that the 2008 crisis hit. Fortunately, he has been able to withstand that disaster.

One of the biggest learnings members take away from their sessions is the importance of not relying on a small number of customers or, as in some cases, one major source of revenue. The 2008 crash saw a number of businesses crumble because major banks and other financial operations suddenly ceased their contracts. A perennial problem with small businesses, as they grow, is that they need to spread their risk; but during that growth period, due to lack of resources, whether money or people, they fail to make the change.

One company that recognised this as an important issue was led by Mike M, who at age 32 was backed by venture capitalists to lead an MBO in the construction industry. He came to the group, which had been going for some time, in 2000. Turnover then was in the low teens of millions. Astute management has enabled that group of companies to grow to around £120 million and has five members of the top team, including the group MD, in various peer groups. As well as learning the importance of leadership versus management, he learned the value and some of the techniques for personal development.

Fred S runs an international fish importing business, bringing in supplies of fresh fish from over 40 countries to leading supermarkets from its location in south-east England. Fred told me that using the concepts learned in the session on Unlocking Creativity™ he was able to effect a huge cultural change in the attitudes of the team, thus grow the business much faster than he had been doing and at the same time enjoy a much more active non-business life. This workshop, fully explained in the next chapter, grew out of the need for peer group members to think differently.

Jerry B had been a long-term member of two such groups. I first met him when he was running a relatively successful travel business focused on the Southern Hemisphere. Travel was, and is, in his blood. He too writes poetry. He recites an amazing poem he wrote to every new member of the team to show them how his passion drives the business and how he wants them to be as passionate about the business as he is. He sold that business very successfully in 2003. After a while he set up a new smaller niche travel business. He has recently sold that business and now operates as a fixer for other travel companies, having emigrated to New Zealand. Hearing and learning from his peers was, he says, instrumental in his success owing to the regular challenges he received.

RA joined the group in 2002. At that time, he was running the brewing subsidiary of a listed company in the East of England. The group CEO role was becoming vacant but he didn't feel that he had the qualities needed to take up that post. He was challenged and encouraged by the group to put his hat in the ring and succeeded in being appointed. Always moderately successful this company has moved forward by leaps and bounds as a FTSE 250 member under his leadership.

One member, Brian M, is a marvel. When the Berlin Wall came down, having operated at the bar coding end of logistics for some time, he had the idea of backing individuals in several Central European countries to set up businesses where he would take a 49% stake and help them to grow. After considerable effort, he has now got their overall agreement to a combined sale to be effected within a relatively short time. The peer group backing has helped him keep his nerve over a number of years, while 'partners' kept changing their minds.

He is a man of huge stamina, riding his bicycle in the non-professional Tour de France, being a magistrate and – his latest venture – having been elected to serve as a local councillor, with the vision of creating a 'smart town'.

I remember one member well. He changed my attitude towards business dress. I came from a background of bowler hats, pin-striped suits and rolled umbrellas. Chris B was a manufacturing jeweller specialising in diamonds whose idea of business dress was a black T-shirt. The dress code for the group became 'come as you please' after he joined. Apart from his main business he bought the subsidiary of an international coin dealer, which specialised in gold bullion. He bought this for a song just before the gold price soared to almost 2,000 US dollars an ounce.

Another member, Paul S, who was with us for eight years, was given a roasting at his first meeting. He already had one 50:50 shareholder and was about to bring someone else in who, it appeared to the group, was going to take him for a ride, expecting equity in return for some quite unclear promises on the sales and marketing side. He took notice of the danger of that but not of the risks in having a 50:50 partner with no shareholders' agreement, a situation that remains to this day.

I had learned a powerful but probably apocryphal lesson many years before about the husband and wife who were 50:50 owners. Their accountant had suggested that this could cause problems in the future and advised them that they should each give 1% to their son, which they duly did. A short while later, the son ganged up with his mother and with 51% together they fired the father!

Inevitably within groups there is a broad spectrum not only of businesses but also of the people who run them. As I've said before, business people join groups but human beings turn up with all their strengths and weaknesses. The group and its interventions help the CEO, the owner manager and the senior executive to succeed, when otherwise they might fail.

So far, all I've talked about is men, this is because for a long time the business environment I was in was one where there were very few women, and those that were tended to be ancillary staff rather than partners or directors.

The first woman I worked with in a senior role was a lawyer Diana D who joined the stockbroking firm (in the 1970's) to beef up our corporate finance team. Whenever we met with potential clients it was always deemed necessary to explain that the pretty blonde wasn't a secretary; she was probably one of the fiercest negotiators you were likely to meet.

Another fearsome negotiator, a speaker on the circuit and a one-time member of one of the Yorkshire-based groups, is Jo Haigh, who trained as both an accountant and lawyer. She has her own corporate finance operation in Wakefield and London, is an author of a multitude of books on directors' roles and duties and is another woman for whom much applause should be given. For fun she and I did a double act at Coutts Bank on the subject of women on boards and at senior levels in business. I played the dumb-assed male stooge!

Other women who have been members or who are still members have included those in recruitment, life sciences, veterinary nursing school, contemporary art gallery, educational research, coaching and training, sports club management, commercial web design, directory publications, branding, accounting and tax, trade magazine publishing. The addition of women to groups, even when in the minority, adds a completely different dimension to the deliberations. It is not necessarily that they are more risk-averse than the men. There is, however, a leaning towards more in not-for-profit and charities.

It can be seen that membership of a mastermind or peer group can offer powerful help to the person in business. Running a business, however much passion you have for the product or service, requires help, be it in recruitment, in developing the necessary processes, always keeping up to date with the latest legislation, developing the appropriate strategy and even helping you develop your vision. Members learn from each other as well as from the speakers and their chair. Even with a fully constituted board of directors, the mixing with others running businesses, whether they be similar in size or entirely different, can bring hugely helpful insights, thus enabling the business leader to move forward faster and more effectively, enabling him or her to build an entity robust enough to be sold or passed to the next generation. New member Mark B, CEO of a leading college of further education – there to ensure the college prospers as a business as well as providing first-class teaching – told me that when he came away from his first group meeting he "felt invigorated, liberated and enthused". He saw that the issues around the table were similar to his; that the members expressed their views "clinically and incisively".

Unlocking Creativity™

Ok, Unlock that Creativity
Why?
Why not?
To elevate the brain upwards
Sideways
Outwards
Inwards
Making left brain stretch
To its outer limits
To the zenith
To the infinite
And how?

By employing right brain
Synthesis
Right brain softness
Right brain luminosity
Making the mind tremble
With virtuosity
With innovation
With sound
Sense
And silence
The stretch
To the ultra-mind.

CHAPTER TWELVE

Unlocking Creativity™

A workshop to exercise the mind, to use
the whole brain to solve problems and
help to drive innovation for profit.

Introduction to the concept

About five years ago, I sat down to write about this subject.
A transcript of one of the workshops I do on Unlocking
Creativity™ was intended to form a book. The draft has been
languishing on Lulu.com ever since! Lulu appeared to me to
be a most helpful website for self-publishing. However, after
one person told me it was unpublishable in that form, I gave
up until now. So it's been banging around my brain ever since I
was turned on to poetry as I explained in the opening chapter.
This successor to 'Poetry in Business' is no longer a turn-off,
particularly in the US. On reflection it's possibly not difficult
to market the concept here in the UK, it's just that I don't get

passionate about marketing. I don't enjoy the process. I am told that I have a 'hurry up' gene so, if I can't see the finished concept, I am probably too lazy to start. That's why I needed a real push to write this book, which I've been getting from Mindy G-K who takes no prisoners! Perhaps I don't explain the benefits enough. The golden rule is benefits not features, but here, I need to talk about the features and then I'll have a crack at the benefits to you, your companies and to your people. You might like to try the exercises as you read through.

So, what's it all about, this Unlocking Creativity™? It's about getting at the truth in yourself and no, it's not all touchy-feely. It can really be quite cathartic and at the same time practical. At a recent workshop, James N, a football-playing, hard-drinking insurance claims underwriter with a finely honed analytical brain, told everyone that before that morning he always thought poetry was sh*t. Yes, I know everyone writes four-letter words these days but I'm still a bit old-fashioned. This is in contrast to Paul B, who left his fire safety business, cleared off to Key West and has published his first novel, one of a trilogy, he says, called *Island on a Sea of Alcohol*. For some reason, he has taken a female nom de plume. Perhaps he fancies himself as a latter day JK Rowling but the book is more like *Fifty Shades of Grey*! Not that I've read that one but one can't help hearing a great deal about it.

The rational and the irrational

Back to the subject of this chapter. In business, as in life, we tend to be very left-brained, very rational thinking. In 2007, Alfa Romeo produced a limited edition of what they called the Alfa 147 Collezione. This was illustrated by an ad in the *Sunday Times* (and presumably elsewhere). A full-page picture shows 'left side of brain' £13,950 and 'right side of brain' a photo of this rather beautiful small car. It even used the words "Use your whole brain". The overall concept described here, is to switch on the right brain so that we use all the brain and not just half of it, so that we are thinking in a holistic way. This enables us to see things far more clearly, to answer the questions we don't even attempt to ask ourselves. This will help to clear the fog that we don't even know is there.

The workshop that I call Unlocking Creativity™ was spawned, as I explained earlier, from a series of 'poetic happenings' that made me realise the truth of what I was saying. Most business people with whom I've worked on this arrive with a huge amount of scepticism but thankfully come away with a perspective that is the result of a complete change of mind. In addition to the guy who said it changed his life and the woman, who reckoned it was the best workshop she'd attended in seven years, it has resonated with a huge number of people, many against their better judgement; but my contention is that once your mind has been affected by the process you cannot help yourself. Even if you don't actually use the system regularly, the way you look at things will be different. Originally it was designed as a peer group workshop but can be, and has been, used in all sorts of different environments ranging from corporate to SME to not-for-profit.

There are a number of well-known people, who are thought of primarily as artists, who have come from a hard-bitten business world, or in some cases, are still there. As I mentioned earlier, we only have to think of Damien Hirst, whose work as an artist is highly controversial but who has a keen eye for profit and knows how to exploit it; there are even business school courses based on his business success in the art market.

We only have to consider his strategy over his diamond skull to realise that he is using his whole brain.

On September 15 and 16 2008, Hirst broke all rules of the art market. He bypassed conventional distribution channels – dealers and gallery owners – by directly partnering with Sotheby's auction house and with their help successfully sold more than 200 pieces of his work. Sotheby's auctioned works of art that were less than two years old, which was another break from tradition. Hirst earned more than £110 million from the auction – in the midst of a global economic crisis and on the same day that Lehman Brothers collapsed.

Paul Gauguin had been a stockbroker. Jeff Koons, a great contemporary sculptor, has been a commodity trader and TS Eliot, an investment banker. One wonders if *The Waste Land* was autobiographical. *The Love Song of J Alfred Prufrock* must have been! Banksy the graffiti artist is extremely creative, extremely clever. He 'gave away' his art on walls until suddenly a market was created. He still cloaks himself in mystery, unlike Tracey Emin who has made a business of being an *enfant terrible* with her art works. It's all about being innovative, about doing things differently. Everyone's 'favourite entrepreneur', the boss of Virgin Airways, Richard Branson, in his motivational book *Screw It, Let's Do It*, says, "do something different each day."

Steve Jobs of Apple fame apparently wrote poetry but, allegedly, according to his biographer, he was on acid at the time. Ron Collins, the founder of WCRS the ad agency, who died in 2013, is reputed to have said that, "nothing of any value is ever created by reasonable people. Poetry, he said, is not reasonable, it comes from the gut." By using or making poetry, we can be irrational and thus creative and innovative. There lies the path to a healthy bottom line.

Ron and his company are famous for:

- *Joan Collins and Reginald Perrin and the Cinzano ad*
- *"it's less bovver than a hover" for Qualcast*
- *ads for Carling Black Label and the spoof ads for Levi's Jeans.*

On the other hand, Aldous Huxley, most famous as the writer of *Brave New World* in 1932, said, "I have discovered the most exciting, the most arduous literary form of all, difficult to master, the most pregnant in curious possibilities. I mean the advertisement. It is far easier to write ten passably effective sonnets, good enough to take in the not too enquiring critic, than one effective advertisement that will take in a few thousand of the uncritical buying public." Of course, advertising has changed not a little since Huxley's day but the point remains well made.

I started off this book suggesting that in business as else-where, we need to combine the numbers, the words and the questions. Ludwig Wittgenstein, the famous Austrian philosopher (1889–1951) said, "the limits of my language are the limits of my mind, all I know is what I have words for." Joseph Epstein, the essayist (born Chicago, 1937) asks, "where do the words come from? The same mysterious place, I suspect where the notes of music go. They precede ideas and are inseparable from them. For myself, I bow my head, touch wood and utter a small prayer that the flow of them never cease."

The *Sunday Times* in February 2005 wrote, "Imagine how the quality of corporate life would improve if chief executives used poetry to galvanize their staff instead of meretricious mission statements."

Music, drama and painting are all ways to achieve what we're trying to suggest here. This is true and effective, but poetry has other attributes too. Lord Byron, the 19th century romantic poet, had a number of children, only one of whom was legitimate; Ada Lovelace (1815–1852). She is credited in computing circles with being the world's first programmer – more than 100 years before the first computer was actually built. Inspired by Charles Babbage's (1791–1871) design for what he called an 'analytical engine', which was never built, she conceived of algorithms that would make the machine capable of many different tasks depending on the routines it was asked to perform. For Lovelace, computing was a marriage of art and science. It was her mother who forced her to be a mathematician to prevent her becoming a poet!

Poetry helps you ask the difficult questions by encapsulating huge ideas in a very simple and succinct way. Unlike prose, it is made up of the minimum of words to get the point made, to get the point over and to drive the bottom line. That's one reason why I've topped each chapter with a poem. Poetry helps you ask the questions you are not asking yourself, the ones you know you should be asking, both in business and in life; as Susan Scott puts it, those 'Fierce Questions', the ones that touch your soul. This is something that is reflected in the poem by the Canadian woman who styles herself Oriah Mountain Dreamer – Native American Elder. *The Invitation*[9] is reproduced here by kind permission. I conclude each Unlocking Creativity™ workshop with this, which to me gets to the real essence of being. It never fails to arouse the emotions of even the hardest bitten business people.

---

[9] *by Oriah Mountain Dreamer from her book 'The Invitation' © 1999.*
Published by Harper Collins/Thorsons. All rights reserved.

The Invitation

It doesn't interest me what you do for a living.
I want to know what you ache for, and if you dare to dream of meeting
your heart's longing.

It doesn't interest me how old you are.
I want to know if you will risk looking like a fool for love, for your
dreams for the adventure of being alive.

It doesn't interest me what planets are squaring your moon,
I want to know if you have touched the center of your own sorrow, if you have been
opened by life's betrayals or have become shriveled and closed from further pain.

I want to know if you can sit with pain, mine or your own, without moving to
hide or fade it or fix it.

I want to know if you can be with joy, mine or your own, if you can dance with
wildness and let the ecstasy fill you to the tips of your fingers and toes without
cautioning us to be careful, be realistic, or to remember the limitations of
being human.

It doesn't interest me if the story you are telling me is true.
I want to know if you can disappoint another to be true to yourself, if you can
bear the accusation of betrayal and not betray your own soul.

I want to know if you can be faithful and therefore be trustworthy.

I want to know if you can see beauty even if it's not pretty every day, and if you can
source your life from its presence.

I want to know if you can live with failure, yours and mine, and still stand on
the edge of a lake and shout to the silver of a full moon, "Yes."

It doesn't interest me to know where you live or how much money you have.
I want to know if you can get up after a night of grief and despair weary and
bruised to the bone, and to do what needs to be done for the children.

It doesn't interest me who you are, or how you came to be here.
I want to know if you will stand in the center of the fire with me and not shrink back.

It doesn't interest me where or what or with whom you have studied.
I want to know what sustains you from the inside when all else falls away. I want to
know if you can be alone with yourself, and if you truly like the company you
keep in the empty moments.

Charles Mingus, great American jazz musician and civil rights activist (born 1922, died 5 January 1979) said, "Anyone can make the simple complicated. Creativity is making the complicated simple." Albert Einstein (Germany 1879 to US 1955) said something similar. He also said, "doing the same thing over and over and expecting different result is the first sign of madness." How many of us are guilty of that, of making the same mistakes over and over? Always make new mistakes!

We've said that asking the difficult questions, asking the daft questions is most important in driving businesses. This came from the University of Pennsylvania psychology department:

Q: What is the secret of your success?
A: Two words.

Q: What are they?
A: Right decisions.

Q: How do you make right decisions?
A: One word.

Q: What is that?
A: Experience.

Q: How do you get experience?
A: Two words.

Q: What are they?
A: Wrong decisions.

By using poetry, combined with the questions, we drive innovation, which feeds directly to the bottom line. It helps create the rhythm, and notice I used the word rhythm and not rhyme. In my opinion poetry does not have to rhyme, although it can do; it doesn't have to scan, like the sort of stuff that was instilled into many of us at school. My view is that it just has to flow like your breathing; you just let it out. I have not met anyone who, if they just let go, can't produce something very meaningful. It's the meaning that we look at, the import, the force, the power that poetry can engender. In the workshop I use a number of well-known and not-so-well-known poems to help create the right atmosphere, to help the delegates get into the mood. One of them, which I found in a book entitled *Ten Poems to Change Your Life* by Roger Housden, was written by Nobel Laureate, Derek Walcott (born St Lucia 1930) and is called 'Love After Love'. Read it before you ask what a 'love' poem is doing in a business seminar. You'll soon see why and it never ceases to gratify me what follows time after time from those in the room.

Love After Love
by Derek Walcott

The time will come
when, with elation,
you will greet yourself arriving
at your own door, in your own mirror,
and each will smile at the other's welcome.

and say, sit here. Eat.
You will love again the stranger who was yourself.
Give wine. Give bread. Give back your heart
to itself, to the stranger who has loved you

all your life, whom you ignored
for another, who knows you by heart.
Take down the love letters from the bookshelf,

the photographs, the desperate notes,
peel your own image from the mirror.
Sit. Feast on your life.[10]

I mentioned at the start of this book that one of the influences that brought me to poetry in business is David Whyte. Again, a very powerful example of his work is used to drive the consciousness of delegates; it is called 'Faith'. It is very short, emphasising the power of a few well-chosen words:

Faith

by David Whyte

I want to write about faith
about the way the moon rises
over the cold snow, night after night,

faithful even as it fades from fullness,
slowly becoming that last curving and impossible
sliver of light before the final darkness.

But I have no faith in myself
I refuse it the smallest entry.

let this then, my small poem,
like a new moon, slender and barely open
be the first prayer that opens me to faith.[11]

---

[10] *Love After Love, from Collected Poems 1948–1984 by Derek Walcott,*
©*1986 by Derek Walcott. Reprinted by permission of Farrar, Strauss and Giroux, LLC.*

[11] *Faith* ©*David Whyte, printed with permission from Many Rivers Press, Langley, Washington*
www.davidwhyte.com

On the other hand, poetry can be used in a very left-brained way, as we've seen in the poem about Pi on page 32.

Poetry in another sense can be used as a great motivator or so it seems. Shakespeare wrote the most wonderful and amazing words in the English language. Motivation is one of the hardest tasks that business leaders have to contend with. Henry V, the night before Agincourt, had to come up with something to motivate his soldiers. He realised that the 10,000 English were hugely outnumbered by 40,000 French troops and were in a sorry state with foot rot, dysentery and other miseries. He went round the camp that night in disguise listening to what his men were saying. The next day he roused them with the following, to my mind one of the greatest motivational pieces ever written:

A Motivational Poem

From Henry V Act 3 Scene 1 – King Henry enters and speaks to his massed troops:

Once more unto the breach, dear friends, once more,
Or close the wall up with our English dead.
In peace there's nothing so becomes a man
As modest stillness and humility,
But when the blast of war blows in our ears,
Then imitate the action of the tiger,
Stiffen the sinews, conjure up the blood,
Disguise fair nature with hard-favoured rage.
Then lend the eye a terrible aspect,
Let it pry through the portage of the head
Like the brass cannon...
Now set the teeth and stretch the nostril wide,

Hold hard the breath, and bend up every spirit
To his full height. On, on, you noblest English,
Whose blood is fet from fathers of war-proof,
Fathers like so many Alexanders
Have in these parts from morn till even fought
And sheathed their swords for lack of argument.
Dishonour not your mothers, now attest
That those you did call fathers did beget you...
        And you, good yeomen,
Whose limbs were made in England, show us here
The mettle of your pasture; let us swear
That you are worth your breeding – which I doubt not
For there is none of you so mean and base
That hath not noble lustre in your eyes.
I see you stand like greyhounds in the slips,
Straining upon the start. The game's afoot.
Follow your spirit, and upon this charge
Cry, "God for Harry! England and Saint George!"

My first rumination on poetry in business, an experiment in every way, was a poem I called 'Corporate Poetry – Getting to the Point'. It's not a very good poem but I got it published in the *London Accountant*, probably the first example of such a juxtaposition. I was, however, chairman of the editorial board at the time!

Corporate Poetry
Getting to the Point

Poetry flows
Poetry connects
Poetry communicates
Its joys and woes
To an ever increasing and ever
Voracious group of individual souls

Manic issues evolved over long frayed
Tantrums in the night and day
Of corporate life can be
And are
Distilled, fumigated, analysed and
Even resolved by forcing them
Elegantly through the sieve of
Heartfelt poetry

The poetry of the immovable
Juxtaposed with the poetry of the solution
Solved, determined, extracted,
Alive.

A much better 'business poem' was written by American poet and businessman, James A Autry (b. Mississippi, 1933). It is called 'Recessions'.

Recessions

Why do we keep on keeping on,
in the midst of such pressure,
when business is no good for no reason,
when the Fed does something
and interest rates do something
and somebody's notion of consumer confidence does something
and the dogs won't eat the dog food?

What keeps us working late at night
and going back every morning,
living on coffee and waiting for things to bottom out,
crunching numbers as if some answer
lay buried in a computer

and not out among the people who
suddenly and for no reason
are leaving their money in their pockets
and the products on the shelves?

Why don't we just say screw it
instead of trying again,
instead of meandering into somebody's office
with half an idea,
hoping he'll have the other half,
hoping, what sometimes happens will happen,
that thing, that click, that moment

when two or three of us
gathered together or hanging out
get hit by something we've never tried
but know we can make work the first time?

Could that be it,
that we do all the dull stuff
just for those times
when a revelation rises among us
like something borning,
a new life, another hope
like something not visible catching the sun,
like a prayer answered?

James A Autry *b.1933 Author, Poet, Lecturer,*
Management Consultant

Another, by a Brit this time, William Ayot (called 'A Doodle at the Edge').

A Doodle at the Edge [12]

Another meeting, another agenda, another
list of buzz-words, initials and initiatives
PSU is entering Phase Three
while the CDR wants G2 to go to Level Five.

If we go the full nine yards on this one;
if we get pro-active, get out of the box, get
our teams together and on the same hymn-sheet;
if we hit the ground running, if we downsize HR,
if we get the money on board, and our asses into gear;
then we can change something, make a difference,
change what the other guys changed last week.

Meanwhile the God has left the garden,
the muse lies minimised in the corner of our screens.
not dead, not buried, but ignored and unseen,
like a doodle at the edge of an action plan.

Me? I say make a sacrifice to the doodle;
pick some flowers, speak a poem, feed the tiny muse.
draw, paint, sing or dance, and you'll bring the gods
back into the board room; the laughing, smiling,
weeping gods of the night-time and the wild.

William Ayot

William is truly a business poet and coach, using poetry in leadership training. He often works with Richard Olivier of Mythodrama, son of Sir Lawrence Olivier. Richard uses Shakespeare and other greats to look at the extraordinary stories in literature and applies them to business. One of his most stirring books is *Inspirational Leadership* first published in 2001, which itself focuses on Henry V as a most inspirational leader.

---

[12] *Doodle at the Edge by William Ayot; from 'Small Things That Matter'*
Published by The Well at Olivier Mythodrama Publishing

In life we unconsciously follow the rules. Earlier we referred to house purchase, car purchase, the biggest personal financial decisions we make, where we tend to be directed by the right brain. Incidentally, from a scientific point of view, researchers at the University of Utah claimed to debunk all left- and right-brained theory in 2013. In my view that does not need to worry us. Continuing to use left/right as a metaphor for rational/creative works for what we are looking at, whether it is physically one side of the brain or not that makes the decision is not necessarily relevant. It's the fact that emotions, unreasonableness, take us over in decision making that is important.

Thus we try and rationalise but the irrational takes over. This also happens in business where we want to recruit someone; for example, we look at the CV, look at what they've achieved and then, do we like them or not. They too are using their gut to see if they want to work with us.

Even in the cold light of day, in the strategy workshop, we need to use gut feeling when eliminating the ideas that we don't feel will work. If we can switch from left to right, if we can combine left and right but not necessarily in the analytical way described in Chapter 3 when discussing Edward De Bono's process of six thinking hats, if we can use the whole brain, how much more powerful will we find our thinking processes to be? By using the techniques described here, and I mean really using them, in a way that makes them part of our daily process, that makes them a habit (using the 30-day technique, described in Chapter 8), we will soon be an automatic creative thinker. When that happens, we will see the realities far more quickly, we will be far more innovative and this, in turn, will help us to grow in business as in life.

The workshop

The workshop starts with a number of simple poems illustrating different facets of the process, following which we then undertake some exercises, one of which asks the delegates to analyse their general work load between several categories; the reason for this is that on most occasions we're going to use the workshop to open the eyes of business leaders to fresh consciousness:

Process	% Time spent	
1. Leading		
2. Managing		
3. Strategy		
4. Sales & Marketing		
5. Administration		

Many do not appreciate, until they face it in this way, just how much time they're spending on items 2 and 5. How much time you spend on item 4 will depend on the size and shape of the business but 1 and 3 should really take up 60% to 70% if not more. Take the test and see where you fit in this patterning, feel where you should be, set a goal for it and just as in the chapter on goals and targets work out by when you're going to get there and then just how you're going to get there. Then set a plan. The techniques described here will help you do just that. This will help counter the argument that 'I have no time.'

The exercises here will help you to identify the very essence, the real core of an individual issue or problem. We tend to call them issues as this avoids negative or blocking connotation. We can then use our findings as a springboard to action and as an aid to communication.

Logic and left-brain thinking does, of course, work, but in many cases it just doesn't; we get blocked or we don't realise just how much further the use of a creative process can take us. As I've said before, we don't know what we don't know; so, let's find out what we don't know! The workshop primes individuals to develop their key plan for their own and their business's progression. Whether personal or in relation to business, the use of poetry and allied exercises will provide the stimulus to get things done. The planning process that follows comes from the heart and mind; it has therefore, true ownership. Gary Hamel, visiting professor, London Business School, author of *Leading the Revolution*, says, "innovation in management principles and processes can create long-lasting advantage and produce dramatic shifts in competitive position." So, we even have an academic on our side!

"This work," according to Chris Hughes, peer group chair in South London and Kent, and himself a speaker on brand positioning and marketing, referring to Unlocking Creativity™, "challenges and stimulates, taking [members] into areas of thinking and feeling that many have never before explored."

Quotations to consider

After the time test, in the workshop, we look at a page of quotations and ask which of them resonate and delegates are then asked to share their thoughts with a colleague around the table. The quotes start to set the mood. They range from:

> *"Going to work for a large company is like getting on a train. Are you going at 60 mph or is the train going 60 mph and you're just standing still?"*
>
> **J Paul Getty**

– I don't think it needs to be a large company, it could just be life.

> *"Do not let what you cannot do interfere with what you can do."*
>
> **John Wooden,** basketball coach.

> *"Few things help an individual more than to place responsibility upon him and to let him know you trust him."*
>
> **Booker T Washington,** Scientist.

> *"Every new product goes through three stages: it won't work... it will cost too much... I thought it was a good idea all the time."*
>
> **Anon.**

Not only do we ensure that people consider the quote that jumps out at them (and there are about two dozen on the page), we make the partner listen very carefully and report back what they've heard. It can sometimes be a huge challenge for them just to listen when they're working out what to say for themselves.

Word exercises

We then move on to some word exercises in order to further limber them up for what comes later. We brainstorm words that motivate, and words that inhibit. It's very interesting that in most cases during these workshops, inhibiting words come out much more quickly than motivating words, a lesson in itself. The second word exercise is to find alternatives, ten synonyms for each of about five words. Again it is fascinating what comes out and just how many alternatives we end up with in groups of perhaps twelve people. We start with this list, which I simply borrowed from a training book a long time ago.

Original	Write up to ten synonyms
Foolish	
Important	
Sad	
Friend	
Fearful	

Notice how each of these words will tend to resonate with you in different ways depending on your current mood.

After this, a poem that takes the group back to the time issue, *'I Have Arrived'* by California writer about work and life, Natasha Josefovitch, now 87 years old:

I Have Arrived

I have not seen the plays in town
only the computer printouts
I have not read the latest books
only the Wall Street Journal
I have not heard the birds sing this year
only the ringing of phones
I have not taken a walk anywhere
but from the parking lot to my office
I have not shared a feeling in years
but my thoughts are known to all
I have not listened to my own needs
but what I want I get
I have not shed a tear in ages
I have arrived
Is this where I was going?

Present and future reality

Then comes an exercise that if I told them about it beforehand, they probably wouldn't turn up! I ask them to take a sheet of paper and hold it landscape – what in my schooldays was called horizontal – and split it into three columns. Column 1 is entitled 'Present Reality', column 2 is not headed and column

3 entitled 'Future Reality'. I tell them that they won't be asked to share what's in columns 1 and 3 but that they will be asked to share the result of column 2. I then ask that they think of a situation in business, or in life generally, that they would like to change and to bullet point a description of how it is now in the first column. Having been given a few moments to do that they are then asked to bullet point their ideal situation in the third column, not necessarily point by point but enough to give them a vision of where they want to be.

Do this for yourself.

Present reality		Future reality
•		•
•		•
•		•
•		

Having done that, put one word, just one word, in the centre column, the word that is stopping you getting from where you are now to where you want to be. Don't discard the first word that comes into your head for that is the word on which you must focus, the 'System 1' word as Daniel Kahneman in *Thinking, Fast and Slow* would put it. Having got that word, write on a fresh piece of paper, the words "I want to write about [..........]. The [........] represents the word you have chosen.

I want to write about . . . .

Often the words include 'fear', 'time', 'me'. We've also had 'momentum', 'money', 'laziness'. Most people in this situation are brutally honest with themselves.

Delegates are then given a rendition of *'Love After Love'* to put them in the mood and after that asked to write their poem. They are reminded that unlike when we were at school, poems do not have to rhyme or scan. They can but it's not essential. As I've said before, the poems just have to have a rhythm, a rhythm that flows with one's breathing. Like workshop delegates, you have just fifteen to twenty minutes to write your poem. Try it; see what happens.

Clearly, occasionally, there are individuals who can't or won't try. There are those who start off with "there was a young lady from..." But when they see their compatriots actually taking this all very seriously they too put their heads down. With very few exceptions they are astounded with what they each come up with. They are then asked to share and so they do. Some amazing results ensue.

Here are four from a recent workshop:

ME

(by MB, CEO of a College of Further Education,
a business man not an academic)

It's not all about me is it? Is It?

*I have become something different, but who am I where
have I come from?*

*Where is the boyhood me who ran, laughed, played so
mischievously*

*Where is the young man with purposeful stride, determined
and with youth on his side*

*The angry young man I left behind that fought to survive, the
struggle with self and burning with passion and desire inside*

Belief and Pride

Look at me now still determined, still learning about me, from
me and others and I see and feel the change inside

All this has shaped me thus far, a far cry from the past me as I
look toward the future me

Who am I now, what will I become next?

Excitement, joy, no more fear, doubt or regret

Celebrating with hearty cheer, mischief and fear given way to
belief, compassion, living in the here and now

Acceptant, contented, proud and me

For now!

Momentum

(by CS, CEO of an ultra-high-tech research company)

What's going on?

When I left it was moving

I only popped out

For goodness sake!

Couldn't you see it slowing?

Surely you heard the grinding?

Christ, I can even smell it!

Come on guys, THINK

Fix this machine

Change the bearings

Top up the oil

I'm coming back...

Right, where are we?

Wow, it's moving on its own

When did anyone last push it?

Really???

Well then, there it is...

Momentum!

Ownership

(by AM, CFO, Insurance)

Are we all answerable?

Answerable to all the others, who ask all the time,
Who tell and dictate, who chide and control.

Are we all answerable?

Answerable to ourselves, to us on our own,
Introspection as we ask, our cares to confide.

Are we all answerable?

Answerable to life, how and what we are,
What drives us on, what holds us back?

If then we answer?

We look up for a change, a more positive step,
Causing our thoughts, to stagger from dreams.

Perhaps then, we can call it ours,
When we take charge, when we set out,
Owning ourselves is a freedom in choice.

Blocked

(by NS, CEO of a trade support organisation, a very creative business)

My momentum is blocked by too much opportunity;
By my love of distractions
And willingness to lounge about on a pretty detour.
There are so many lines on my map
That I cannot clearly see the way to our destination.
When I share the vision people briefly glimpse the peak:
It is majestic, snowy-capped and tall.
Come climb with me, I ask,

And they come trusting me.

We enjoy the foothills

And the sense of closing the big target.

But at other times we are less certain:

It is night and we have no torch to see the page.

Are we really going? Yes, I say. Yes.

In part because in thinking of the prize

I have already spent it:

And that's OK.

In longer workshops where we have more time, they are then asked to 'coach' each other on their poems, pulling out the subconscious meaning, in some cases using the 'Fierce Conversations' techniques, being asked questions or using 'clean language' strategy (a coaching technique). This is extraordinarily powerful. They are also asked to type out their efforts and share when going away from the workshop with life and business partners. Again some lovely stories of greater understanding are generated. As each of these is extremely personal, the details must be kept dark, a tenet of Chatham House rules; what is said in the room, stays in the room. This is the key to sharing their most intimate thoughts. For this reason, initials only are used here when detailing some examples.

As has been said before, this technique has been taken to the boardroom, the living room and the bedroom to great and lasting effect. It enables people to understand their partners better, and gives them the deep knowledge to help their mutual development. As we all know development in business and in personal lives is one of the keys to success. This does much more, in my view; it helps people look at themselves and others in a new light and helps them to be more creative, to be more innovative and thus to achieve better results. If, by using these techniques we can change attitudes, our own and others, change cultures, absorb higher values, we will surely reach those higher planes that Maslow talked about.

Pam W used this workshop to inspire her to write a poem to every chief executive whose company owed money to her luxury brand marketing company. She told me that they all paid up within a week!

Subject to the time available, we might talk about timelines, tracing people's highs and lows in career and life generally. We might look at tolerations, where the delegates are asked to write down the things they tolerate in ten categories (five of each) ranging from 'relationship and family' to 'home and office' and 'car, appliances and equipment'. How many light bulbs need changing and yes, I've remembered that old joke about how many software engineers it takes to change a light bulb. Can't be done, it's a hardware problem. Commit to the elimination of the things you tolerate, using your coach where necessary.

A further exercise returns to *Fierce Conversations©*, asking the really deep but always open questions. We often use just six, asking delegates to choose only two but one of which must be number 6. They then share, listen and report as in an earlier exercise.

Six Questions: try them yourself with a partner or colleague.

1. What would you do if you, personally, received £5,000,000 unexpectedly next week?

2. What would you do if you only had six months to live?

3. What do you dream of achieving, attempting or experiencing?

4. What is your greatest fear that holds you back?

5. What one great thing would you dare to dream if you knew you couldn't fail?

6. What is the question you are not asking yourself? *(Compulsory)*

This brings you back to real life but will shake your intellectual skills, your imagination and your ability to be creative. The exercises end with an extract from *The Magic Box*, a children's book, 'Cat Amongst the Pigeons' by Kit Wright.

The Magic Box
by Kit Wright[13]

I will put in the box

the swish of a silk sari on a summer night,
fire from the nostrils of a Chinese dragon,
the tip of a tongue touching a tooth.

I will put in the box
a snowman with a rumbling belly
a sip of the bluest water from Lake Lucerne,
a leaping spark from an electric fish.

I will put into the box
three violet wishes spoken in Gujarati,
the last joke of an ancient uncle,
and the first smile of a baby.

I will put into the box

---

[13] *From 'Cat Amongst the Pigeons', Viking Kestrel, 1987. © Kit Wright 1987*

a fifth season and a black sun,
a cowboy on a broomstick
and a witch on a white horse.
My box is fashioned from ice and gold and steel,
with stars on the lid and secrets in the corners.
Its hinges are the toe joints of dinosaurs.
I shall surf in my box
on the great high-rolling breakers of the wild Atlantic,
then wash ashore on a yellow beach
the colour of the sun.

Describe your box and its contents. Only on one occasion, in Lancaster, Pennsylvania, did one man write, 'my wife, my dog, a bottle of wine'. However, NS wrote:

My box is adamantine with a lid slammed shut.
After a millennium under the Indian Ocean
It is covered with barnacles and coral.
Inside happiness blazes
As oxygen atoms joyfully tear apart the universe
Again and again.
There is music that switches with my anticipated mood
And if you are careful
A generous gift that requires no return.
If only I paid more attention to it!

You have to be daring; as Teddy Roosevelt (1858–1919) 26th president of the United States, said:

"It's not the critic that counts, not the man who points out how the strong man stumbled or where the doer of deeds could have done better. The credit belongs to the man who is actually in the arena; whose face is marred

by dust and sweat and blood; who strives valiantly; who errs and comes short again and again; who knows the great enthusiasms, the great devotions, and spends himself in a worthy cause; who at the best, knows in the end the triumph of high achievement; and who at the worst, if he fails, at least fails whilst daring greatly, so that his place shall never be with those cold and timid souls who know neither victory nor defeat."

Conclusion
– Considering the Combination

Seeing things
In different ways
Seeing things
Through a glass
Brightly
That is running
And driving
The business
To success.
Although we must
See things
From many
Angles
From many
Perspectives, it is all
The one
It is all
The combination
Of those

Perspectives
That will win
The day
That will win
The prize
The development
The success
Of the magical
And magnificent
Prize
By driving forward
With spirited
And spectacular
Process
In an endeavour
That wins the day
In each and every
Way.

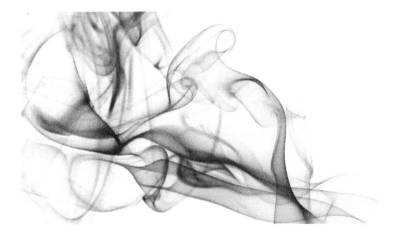

CHAPTER THIRTEEN

Considering the Combination

Getting the right people on board

IN THIS closing chapter, I'm aiming to bring all this together; it's all about the numbers, it's all about the words, it's all about the questions. Peter Thomson uses a modicum of words to talk about numbers and goals and objectives and while doing so asks lots of questions.

So, I'll begin this final chapter with the words and numbers of Peter Thomson, a master at turning information into product. His weekly online newsletter 'Thank God it's Monday', is one of the few I read with regularity. He recently said this:

"It's all in the counting; you and I can learn so much from other people.

"Recently, I saw, on film, a member of AA (Alcoholics not Automobile) state that he was an alcoholic but that he'd been drink-free for 15 years and 264 days. He went on to say – that the number was the factor that kept him sober. Having been sober for so long he just couldn't imagine having to start the count again – from zero! What a lesson this is and... you and I can use it to such good effect in so many areas of our business and personal lives.

"Here's how... Let's say you want to improve a particular skill." Peter quotes a friend, Alex Garcez, who teaches speed-reading who says, "make a promise to yourself that you'll practise for at least **one minute per day**. In the past we've all promised ourselves to practice or do something every day for x amount of time. Then because of some happening or other – we didn't do it one day. The one day became two days and the habit was broken! But **one minute**? Well – that's a promise we can keep EVERY DAY! There's never an excuse to avoid just one minute. And if the one turns into 5 or 10 or 14 even better. But the habit remains in place and the counting starts – and continues.

"I've practised my speed-reading for so many consecutive days (and I'm keeping count) – that I just couldn't bear the idea of going back to zero to start all over again. So I just keep up the habits! Where can you use counting? Answer – everywhere! But specifically, any habit you want to create or maintain. How about writing one sentence of your book – every single day? Just one sentence! How about making a one-minute call to a family member every single day? Just one minute! How about doing one press-up every single day? – Just one!

"Of course, you and I know what'll happen: we'll write more sentences on many days and suddenly the book will be finished. We'll chatter for more than a minute and change someone's life. We'll love the burn and press-up numbers will soar. The kicker, **we must keep count**. That's what makes this work. The magic is in the counting."

Just look at these patterns; I think they're beautiful. They show me why numbers are so powerful.

$$1x8+1=9$$
$$12x8+2=98$$
$$123x8+3=987$$
$$1234\ x8+4=9876$$
$$12345x8+5=98765$$
$$123456x8+6=987654$$
$$1234567x8+7=9876543$$
$$12345678x8+8=98765432$$
$$123456789x8+9=987654321$$

$$1x9+2=11$$
$$12x9+3=111$$
$$123x9+4=1111$$
$$1234x9+5=11111$$
$$12345x9+6=111111$$
$$123456x9+7=1111111$$
$$1234567x9+8=11111111$$
$$12345678x9+9=111111111$$
$$123456789x9+10=1111111111$$

$$9 \times 9 + 7 = 88$$
$$98 \times 9 + 6 = 888$$
$$987 \times 9 + 5 = 8888$$
$$9876 \times 9 + 4 = 88888$$
$$98765 \times 9 + 3 = 888888$$
$$987654 \times 9 + 2 = 8888888$$
$$9876543 \times 9 + 1 = 88888888$$
$$98765432 \times 9 + 0 = 888888888$$

$$1 \times 1 = 1$$
$$11 \times 11 = 121$$
$$111 \times 111 = 12321$$
$$1111 \times 1111 = 1234321$$
$$11111 \times 11111 = 123454321$$
$$111111 \times 111111 = 12345654321$$
$$1111111 \times 1111111 = 1234567654321$$
$$11111111 \times 11111111 = 123456787654321$$
$$111111111 \times 111111111 = 12345678987654321$$

These are not just pretty pictures; they illustrate both the complexity and the simplicity of our number systems. In many ways they show how powerful numbers can be; how they can be used to create a picture that most people can understand, even if they are unable, because of lack of training, to actually put them together. "The brain loves a number," we've said this a few times particularly in relation to goal setting. A goal cannot be reached if it is not described and usually best described by using numbers. We do, of course have many gaols that we describe in non-numerical terms but do they resonate quite as well as when they are expressed numerically? The same applies to KPIs, key performance indicators. How much easier is it to see just where we are if we have numbers to compare. As for questions using numbers: how many? How often? How big? The answers help us to understand. The answers help others to describe, to explain.

Number puzzles

We can easily see how numbers can fit into and challenge our thinking processes. Simple number puzzles can illustrate this phenomenon. Answers can be found in the appendix.

1) *2 drums, 1 holds 5 gallons, the other 3 gallons.*
   How do you measure just 1 gallon?

2) *9 marbles look and feel exactly the same except one is*
   1.1 ounce and the others are exactly 1 ounce.
   You have weighing machine; how do you find which
   is the heavier one in just two weighings?

3) *Add all the numbers from 1 to 100 in an instant.*

4) *Put a mathematical symbol between the numbers 4*
   and 5 to give a number greater than 4 and less than 5.

5) *What odd numbers when added together make 14?*
   All digits must be identical.

6) *A new street is built with 100 houses numbered 1*
   to 100. How many 9s?

7) *A brick weighs 1 kg plus half a brick.*
   How much does a brick weigh?

8) *A bat and a ball together cost £1.10; the bat costs £1 more than the ball. How much does the ball cost?*

9) *If this is a magic word A – – A – A – A – – A; what is this: – A – A – A – A – A – A?*

10) *It takes 5 machines 5 minutes to make 5 widgets. How long does it take 100 machines to make 100 widgets? 5 minutes or 100 minutes?*

11) *In a lake there is a patch of lily pads. Every day the patch doubles in size. If it takes 48 days for the patch to cover the whole lake how long would it take for the patch to cover half the lake?*

12) *111 teams in a knock-out tournament. How many games to find the overall winner? How many losers?*

13) *Bath tub with 3 taps: tap 1 takes 10 minutes to fill the bath; tap 2 takes 20 minutes, tap 3 takes 30 minutes. If all three taps are turned on simultaneously how long to fill the bath?*

These types of problems are simple and difficult simultaneously, they require whole-brain thinking. They're not just rational mathematical problems as they need us to think irrationally at the same time. We have to question the import behind the problem. Thus they encapsulate the whole thesis behind this book, the combination of all three qualities, strengths in business and also in life generally.

The rational, the irrational, the linkage and connection of the two; the checking, the understanding, the meld will help business to thrive, businesses to succeed, owners to reach their ultimate targets, employees to more fully understand what it is that is expected of them. What it is that will help them drive their careers forward at an enhanced rate.

In various parts of this book we've looked at the 'Why?' We've looked at needs and wants, we've looked at benefits over features; all aspects covered many times over the years by many authors. So why did I feel it was necessary to write this book? Does anyone really need it? What's the benefit of reading it? How does anyone know to pick it up and have a go? I've tried to make it an enjoyable read. I've tried to read far too many books and just given up because they had nothing new to say or were just dry and dull. So the poems, the vignettes, the anecdotes, the mini case histories you'll find in here are an attempt to enliven and illustrate a serious business case, to make you want to know more once you've started and to help you be successful in your own businesses.

Tom Hill, of the Eagle Summit and of the networking organisation Arête, has a great method of reading, he says, a book a day! Start with the cover and the author's objectives. Review the list of contents. Read the first and last paragraph of each chapter and if you want to know more then that's up to you. He believes that if you do just that you will find the essence and get out of it what you need. It's for this reason that I've started each chapter with a poem, the aim of which is to partly encapsulate the chapter's contents and partly to act as stimulant to drive you forward so that you'll be able to decide very quickly whether you want to go further. As a new writer of prose, I'm clearly living dangerously!

The overall conclusion is simple but bears repeating. People go into business, start or go in to continue an existing business, because they are passionate about the service or the product that they are going to develop and grow. They need something different, something extra to make it work. Yes, they need the numbers, yes, they need the words and certainly they need to ask the right questions but I contend that they need all three combined, all three simultaneously, all three in play at all times in order to drive success. Not everyone is capable of that conjunction so if not they must ensure that the expertise is brought in otherwise there is a great danger that failure will ensue.

Use the tools we've talked about in this book, the creativity exercises, both the poetry ones and the arithmetical ones; use the tried and tested concepts of those who've done it before and succeeded. Learn to stretch and bend the mind, the whole mind, and see that it is applied in your business, that it is inculcated in your team, which you've selected, with the help of your leadership and your and their continuous learning. Prepare for the future as it will help take you forward.

Succeed!

Appendix

Answers to puzzles from Chapter 13

1) *Fill the three gallon drum, pour into the five; fill the three again; put what you can into the five.*
   There will be one left in the three.

2) *Weigh three in each pan; if it doesn't balance take the heavier three and weigh one in each pan. If they do balance take two of the remaining three.*

3) *50 pairs of 101 = 5050*

4) *4.5*

5) *11, 1, 1, 1*

6) *20 including all the 90s and 99*

7) *2 kg*

8) *5p*

9) *ABRACADABRA and TARAMASALATA*

10) *5 minutes*

11) *47 days*

12) *111-1=110 (or n-1 i.e. whatever the number less 1)*

13) *Approximately 5.4 minutes*

Reading list

Introduction
The E-Myth (and *The E-Myth Revisited*), Michael E Gerber

Chapter 1
The Element, Ken Robinson
The 4-Hour Work Week, Timothy Ferriss

Chapter 2
The Genghis Khan Guide to Business, Brian Warnes
Time to Think, Nancy Kline
The Servant as Leader, Robert Greenleaf
The Balanced Scorecard: Translating Strategy into Action, Robert Kaplan and DP Norton
CEO Tools, Kraig Kramers
Good to Great, Jim Collins
Get a Grip, Gino Wickman & Mike Paton
The Five Temptations of a CEO, Patrick Lencioni
The Five Dysfunctions of a Team, Patrick Lencioni

Chapter 3

The Black Swan, Nassim Nicholas Taleb

The Power of Now, Eckhart Tolle

Six Thinking Hats, Edward de Bono

The Speed of Trust, Stephen MR Covey and Rebecca Merrill

Chapter 5

The Puritan Gift, Kenneth & William Hopper

Know Me, Like Me, Follow Me, Penny Power

Now, Discover Your Strengths, Marcus Buckingham

Chapter 6

Start With Why, Simon Sinek

Selling to VITO, Anthony Parinello

Creating Competitive Advantage, Jaynie L Smith

The Beermat Entrepreneur, Mike Southon and Christopher West

Chapter 7

Fooled by Randomness, Nassim Nicholas Taleb

Chapter 8

Emotional Intelligence, Daniel Goleman

Thinking, Fast and Slow, Daniel Kahneman

Chapter 9

The Business Rules, Jo Haigh

What Got You Here Won't Get You There, Marshall Goldsmith

Chapter 10
How Would You Move Mount Fuji?, William Poundstone

Chapter 11
Think and Grow Rich, Napoleon Hill

Chapter 12
Screw It, Let's Do It, Richard Branson

Inspirational Leadership, Richard Olivier

Leading the Revolution, Gary Hamel

About the Author

DAVID ADAMS is a business and leadership coach and mentor. A chartered accountant, he has been a stockbroker and corporate financier and ultimately chief executive of a major firm. He has acted as a consultant to professional practices and the Stock Exchange, London and interim managed a medical technology company leading to its sale to a listed company. He has held a number of non-executive directorships inter alia in property, publishing, retail, recruitment, and marketing and communications.

David has spent the last decade providing leadership and business coaching to both senior corporate executives and owner managers. He runs CEO and small business groups for Vistage International, the world's leading chief executive peer group organisation.

He is a member of the Association for Coaching. He is a governor of the Kensington and Chelsea College of Further Education and a trustee of CABA, the Chartered Accountants Benevolent Association. He is a former director of the Hampstead Theatre, London and a former president of the London Society of Chartered Accountants.

As an international performance poet he has brought poetry to coaching and training as a means of unlocking creativity and driving innovation in teams and individuals.

Testimonials

I have known David for upwards of 20 years and he is a good friend and colleague at Vistage International. He is a very experienced businessman with high levels of professionalism and commitment. Above all he is a "left field" thinker and a most accomplished poet as well as being a great coach to many MDs and CEOs.

Ivan Goldberg, Executive Mentor & Coach, Manchester

David Adams has an innate ability to get to the heart of the matter and help you find your solution fast. He is a very good coach and has a vast amount of experience that he is able to draw upon in an instant. In an age of fast cars, a million marketing messages a day and '24 hour everything,' he always has time to listen, support and encourage. Through David's sensitive yet challenging approach he helped me find the courage to make some very big life changing decisions. I enthusiastically recommend David to anyone facing change, wants to be challenged and is ready to take their business on to another level.

Lin Dickens, Marketing Director at Inn or Out Events Ltd, London

In seven years of hearing valuable speakers each month, I can say that this was the most valuable, the most resonate, and the most needed workshop I have experienced... and dare I say, that our group experienced. The creativity and power of David's facilitation and process fostered an environment of right-brained, expansive and connected thinking - something that could be difficult to accomplish inside a room full of busy CEOs.

Ash Robinson, Founder at Purpose, Profit and You, San Diego

I have found David a constant source of inspiration and new ideas. He has an uncanny ability to point out the obvious when you can't see it yourself.

Andrew Crawford, New England Seafood International Ltd, Dorchester

David Adams is one of those rare people you will find yourself fortunate to meet and be changed by knowing him. I see David as a thoughtful, always thirsty for learning, Chair of leaders that is ready to take his group on the journey of a lifetime.

Janet Fogarty, Performance Catalyst. Centennial, Colorado, USA

David Adams is a brilliantly articulate and expressive speaker and workshop leader. His work with my Chief Executive Group was both masterful, fun, and transforming. He has the ability to support participants in going deep without eliciting fear or trepidation. He creates an atmosphere of mutual trust, respect and safety in which real learning can take place.

Dwight Frindt, CEO Advisor, Executive Coach & Consultant, Leadership Author, Strategy & Alignment Expert. Kirkland, Washington, USA

David is one of those rare individuals who successfully combines extensive experience of working with the most senior level in large corporate organisations. He has been chief executive, coach, non-executive director, with innovative and creative instincts, and outstanding interpersonal skills.

Martin Gillespie, Owner, Inspire Development and Coaching. Reading

David is an exceptional coach who has the ability to understand and relate to the issues facing executives and a talent for helping people get the best from themselves and their team.

His Unlocking Creativity seminar is a real eye-opener. Who would ever have thought that poetry could be used to in such an interesting way?

Paul Smyth, CEO at Kynetix Technology Group, Croydon

David's work with executives and their teams truly helps unlock the creativity. Dynamic, powerful in bringing out the creative within.

Ozzie Gontang, Master Chair/Mentor/Coach-Vistage Int'l. San Diego, California

His quiet and patient ability to get to the heart of the motivations that drive leaders and businesses is extraordinary. I've discovered more about how to get the best out myself and my team working with David in six months than in the previous few years of running my own business.

Stephen Thorn, Head of Relationships, EY Foundation, Stevenage

Lightning Source UK Ltd.
Milton Keynes UK
UKOW06f0036270615

254215UK00002B/23/P